# THE BOOK OF
# SNAKES

# THE BOOK OF
# SNAKES

## JOHN A. BURTON

CHARTWELL
BOOKS, INC.

Published by Chartwell Books
A Division of Book Sales Inc.
114 Northfield Avenue
Edison, New Jersey 08837
USA

ISBN 0-7858-0952-X

QUMSNA

This book is produced by
Quantum Books Ltd
6 Blundell Street
London N7 9BH

Printed in Singapore by
Star Standard Industries Pte Ltd

# CONTENTS

# SNAKES AND PEOPLE

Snakes have always held a fascination, often bordering on an obsession, for people; and since prehistoric times, they have been shrouded in mysticism and superstition. There are several sites in Europe where snakes appear in Stone Age cave paintings. In a huge cave at Baume Latrone in France, a 10-foot (3-meter) serpent with a clearly defined head, fangs, and tongue is surrounded by diminutive elephants. At Rouffignac, also in France, is the recently discovered Dome of Serpents which contains hundreds of intertwining serpentine lines on its curved clay ceiling. The aborigines in Australia, who still practice rock painting, frequently depict snakes.

This fascination was due, at least partly, to their strange shape and motion, and their ability to strike unexpectedly with deadly accuracy. Such inhuman or "unnatural" attributes led them to be considered supernatural and superhuman. Myths and legends about snakes abound, and they have been worshiped and used in ceremonies and rituals all over the world.

*Adam and Eve (above) being tempted by the snake in a traditional wood carving from Sweden, now in the Nordiskn Museet,*

*Stockholm, Sweden. A Swedish embroidery of Adam and Eve in the Garden of Eden (below), dating from 1812.*

### RITUALS, MYTHS, AND SNAKE WORSHIP

In the Biblical account of the Creation, Adam and Eve are tricked by the serpent in the Garden of Eden into eating the fruit of the tree of knowledge and, consequently, the Judeo-Christian view of the serpent is one of evil. By contrast, in ancient Egypt snakes were revered as gods. Its economy depended on the Nile, and the Spirit of the Nile was a snake god. The hieroglyph of two cobras became the written sign of the two lands of Egypt, and the Pharaoh had a cobra incorporated into his crown, with the snake symbolizing the mighty power of the ruler. One of the most famous snakes of ancient Egypt is the asp supposedly used in the suicide of Cleopatra. This may have been the Egyptian Cobra, *(Naja haje)* or one of the poisonous vipers found in Egypt.

The Babylonians of ancient Mesopotamia also had snake deities. The Euphrates was called the river of the snake, and the fertility of the Earth was symbolized by the snake. The phallic associations of the snake probably played an important part in its selection for use in fertility rituals.

Snakes featured prominently in the classical civilizations of Greece and Rome. Hermes, the messenger of the gods, carried a staff wreathed with twin snakes. Athena, goddess of war and guardian of the city of Athens, had a snake on her shield. Fertility festivals were practiced in Greece, with snakes as part of the sacred ritual. Hercules, a demigod, slew snakes, including the seven-headed snake monster, while Medusa, a monster that turned those who looked at her into stone, had a writhing mass of snakes in place

Osiris as judge of the dead, and Horus presenting the spirit of a dead man , painted on a mummy case from Thebes dating from 900 B.C. and now in the British Museum. The regalia of the Pharaohs included a cobra.

The head of the Gorgon, Medusa, in a Roman mosaic at Dar Zemla, Tunisia, dating from the late A.D. 200s.

of her hair.

The Central American Aztec civilization had a snake god known as Quetzalcóatl, or the feathered serpent, who was the god of civilization. His representation survives on many buildings and temples, including the important temple at Teotihuacán in Mexico. Snakes are also part of the myths, customs, and rituals of the North American Indians. Especially famous is the ritual snake dance of the Hopi tribe in honor of the rattlesnake.

In Asia, snakes are often held in high esteem. In many parts of India, for instance, the cobra is worshiped, and great festivals are held in its honor. It is believed that when a wealthy man dies without an heir, he returns in the form of a serpent to guard his wealth. In other parts of India, it is thought that if a copper coin is placed in the mouth of a dead

snake and the body ceremoniously buried, evil will be averted. In Malaysia, Temple Pit Vipers *(Trimeresurus wagleri)* live in the Buddhist snake temples, where they are looked after by the monks. These poisonous snakes are revered and supposedly bring good fortune.

The python is especially revered in Africa and is very much a part of local myth and superstition. In Zimbabwe, a python must be burned after it has been killed; otherwise, there will be a very long drought. A similar belief exists in South Africa. In Dahomey and Nigeria in west Africa, pythons were worshiped, and people taken from there to the Caribbean as slaves took their religion with them in the form of voodoo, which they practiced in their new countries.

The Australian aborigines have numerous myths and legends concerning snakes. One particularly common myth tells of a snake that

*An Australian aboriginal bark painting (right) from Arnhemland, Australia, depicting a snake with a goanna (monitor lizard), turtle, and birds.*

*Living Temple Pit Vipers (*Trimeresurus wagleri *below) in the Snake Temple at Sungei Kluang on the Malaysian island of Penang, draped around effigies of local deities. The snakes live in semifreedom, looked after by the monks who believe they are endowed with the power of bringing good fortune.*

once lived in a pool and made rain by spitting up into the sky until clouds and a rainbow formed, and the rain began to fall. This rainbow serpent still plays a part in aboriginal rainmaking ceremonies.

## SNAKES IN MEDICINE

Just as snakes figured in myths and legends as symbols of both good and evil, so in medicine they were regarded as sources of maladies and cures. In 293 B.C., there was a plague in Rome, and the Roman god of medicine, Aesculapius, appeared in the form of a snake. The plague disappeared, and a temple was built in his honor. His staff was wreathed in snakes and, even today, the emblem of the medical profession is a staff with two entwined snakes. The snake associated with Aesculapius may have been *Elaphe longissima*, which is now known as the Aesculapian Snake. Its occurrence in isolated scattered colonies in the north of its range may be a result of captives being taken north and kept at Roman temples as sacred animals.

Eating the flesh of snakes is often thought to cure or prevent all manner of diseases. The Chinese eat snakes as a cure for tuberculosis, and rattlesnake oil was sold as a remedy in the U.S.A., while the Romans used snake grease as a hair restorer. Snake venom has been used as a cure for gangrene, meningitis, and cholera, and the dried venom of Russell's Viper *(Vipera russelli)* has been widely used in recent years as a blood coagulant.

In contrast, there were superstitions in olden days that the sight of snakes could make you ill, or even kill you. Diseases were often attributed to snakes or to their spirits in the sick person's body. It was widely believed in medieval Europe, for example, that snakes could enter a sleeping person's mouth and eat their insides, the cure for which was eating garlic.

### SNAKEBITES

The fact that some snakes are highly poisonous has made all snakes widely feared. Even harmless creatures such as the amphisbaenids were thought to be two-headed and extremely poisonous because they are snakelike and have a tail similar to the head. Elaborate precautions were often taken to prevent being bitten by snakes. Cowboys in the Old West often put a hair rope around their camp in the belief that snakes would not cross over it, lest it scratch their bellies. People wore amulets to guard against snakebites; and spells, dances, and ceremonies were performed to obtain protection.

Despite all such precautions, people were, and still are, bitten, and the communities most affected developed remedies, sometimes administered by snake doctors. The most remarkable snake doctors

*Aesculapius, the Roman god of medicine (left), is traditionally depicted with a snake, as in this Roman copy of a Greek sculpture now in the Vatican Museum. It is possible that the distribution of the Aesculapian Snake (Elaphe longissima) was modified by Romans introducing them around the sites of temples.*

*An image of Buddha protected by the hoods of the Naga, a snake deity (below), in the Buddist cave temple at Dambulla, Sri Lanka. In India, snakes including cobras are generally revered rather than persecuted, as in Europe.*

*A Black Mamba* (Dendroaspis polyepis *right) being milked for its venom on a snake farm. The advent of antivenin has reduced the mortality rates from snakebites in most parts of the world. However, in many developing countries, people still tend to use traditional herbal "cures" which are generally ineffective.*

were the Psylli of North Africa and Asia Minor, who were reputed to be able to cure snakebites just by touching the wound with their fingers. Since many snakebite victims probably received relatively small amounts of venom and suffered mainly from acute shock, such calming measures would have stood a reasonable chance of success. Other traditional remedies for snakebites include eating the snake itself, leeches and bleeding to remove the contaminated blood, using porous stones to draw out the blood, using plants as antidotes, and putting gunpowder on the wound and exploding it. Yet another is the use of alcohol in great quantity. It is said that an American man who had been bitten by a rattlesnake was given one and a half gallons of whiskey and a quart of brandy as a remedy. It was allegedly so successful that the man went out the next day to find another rattlesnake to bite him! This seems unlikely because alcohol is one of the worst things a snakebite victim can be given. In fact, there is little evidence that the majority of the herbal and other traditional remedies actually work, and in those countries where people still trust in them, deaths from snakebites are common.

The development of effective treatments for snakebites only really began in the late nineteenth century. In 1887, G. Sewall published the results of his work on preventive inoculation. When experimental animals were repeatedly injected with sublethal doses of rattlesnake venom, they gradually built up a resistance and became immune to a lethal dose. This work was built on by the Pasteur Institute, which discovered that previously untreated animals could be protected by injecting them with the blood of animals immunized by Sewall's method. This led to the idea of using the blood serum of an immunized animal

as an antidote to snakebite poisoning. Antivenom serum, or antivenin, was a resounding success and, in 1895, antivenin was used for the first time on a human being. A few years later, commercial production began of antivenin against cobra bites produced from horses, and institutes were set up for the research, production, and distribution of antivenin.

Today, in snake farms from Thailand to Brazil, large numbers of snakes are "milked" for their venom, which is used in the production of serum. It was once hoped to produce a single antivenin for all snakes, but this proved impossible. It was then thought that venoms could be divided into two groups – neurotoxins (affecting nerves) and hemotoxins (affecting blood). However, venoms were found to be much more complicated, varying not only between different groups of snakes, but also within different individuals of the same species. So, several antivenins are used together to treat the bites of a number of possible snakes found in any one area.

It is estimated that about 30,000 humans die each year as a result of snakebites, mostly in poorer countries with few medical facilities. In India, 10,000-12,000 people die annually, whereas in the U.S.A. an average of less than 30 people die each year and many of them actually handle snakes. In Britain, there were seven deaths from Adder (viper) bites between 1899 and 1945, only one between 1945 and 1960, and none recorded in recent years. Indeed, in Britain you are much more likely to be killed by or with horses (21 deaths in 1983), or by bee and wasp stings (6 deaths in 1983).

With a few simple precautions, bites can be prevented. Such precautions include not picking up unidentified snakes, being careful where you walk, and wearing adequate footwear. Snakebite kits are often available in areas with poisonous snakes, but the effectiveness of such kits is questionable. Also, some antivenins, if wrongly administered, can be more dangerous than some snakebites.

### SNAKE CHARMING AND SNAKE DANCING

Snake charming is part of everyday entertainment in north Africa and, especially, India. Cobras are often used, especially the King Cobra *(Ophiophagus hannah)* and the Spectacled Cobra *(Naja naja)*, and there is a great deal of mystery surrounding the techniques involved. The snakes cannot hear the music played by the charmer and are held in strike pose, with head raised and hood expanded, by the movements of the charmer's hands and pipe. The charmers rely heavily on their knowledge of snake behavior, but do sometimes get bitten, sometimes fatally, and this is considered an occupational hazard. Some charmers protect themselves by knocking the fangs out or making the snake strike repeatedly until it has exhausted its venom. The charmer may kiss the cobra on the head, but this is perhaps not quite as dangerous as it looks, since snakes can only strike downward, forward, and from some distance away.

Other performers arrange fights between a snake and a mongoose. The snake is usually killed, as everybody who has read Rudyard Kipling's story of Rikki Tikki Tavi in *The Jungle Book* would expect. In India and Japan, performers put a live snake in the nostril and bring it out through the mouth. Snake dancing has its origins in India, and very different dances with snakes are now performed by cabaret and striptease artists

around the world. Usually, nonaggressive and nonpoisonous snakes such as the Indian Python *(Python molurus)* and the Boa Constrictor *(Boa constrictor)* are used. Roadside rattlesnake shows used to be held in the U.S.A.

Snakes are commonly kept in zoos, mainly as spectacles, although some zoos have had successful breeding programs. In some wildlife sanctuaries, such as the famous Australian Reptile Park in New South Wales or the Madras Snake Park in India, there are public reptile demonstrations. Visitors are allowed to handle snakes, as well as learning about snakebites and the lifesaving role the parks play in the production of antivenins.

*An Indian snake charmer (below), photographed on the streets of Delhi with a cobra. Snake charmers rely on their movements to "hypnotize" the snake, since snakes are deaf and cannot hear the music which is played as part of the performance.*

# EVOLUTION AND BIOLOGY

Long before humans and other mammals evolved, reptiles were spreading over all but the coldest parts of the world. Although the loss of their limbs might seem a disadvantage, snakes are a highly successful group of reptiles that have managed to colonize almost all habitats since they appeared at least 130 million years ago.

Snakes have a number of features in common, making their biology rather consistent. Their long, cylindrical bodies impose restrictions, and all snakes are to a greater or lesser extent dependent on the warmth of the sun to maintain their body temperature and to incubate their eggs or develop the young.

Although some species are territorial, some have elaborate courtships and others hibernate communally, snakes generally lack the social behavior found in many birds, mammals, and other groups of animals.

*The Paradise Flying Snake* (Chrysopelea paradisa *left), photographed in a Malaysian rain forest. One of the most attractively marked snakes, its very distinctive pattern camouflages it well amid the contrasting shadows and light of its forest habitat.*

# ANCESTRY AND EVOLUTION

The main clues to the evolution of creatures come from the preserved remains or fossils of their ancestors, found in the rocks. The earliest fossil remains recognizable as being a snake were found in Lower Cretaceous (130-million-year-old) rocks in the Sahara, North Africa. The most complete and significant fossil find was from Upper Cretaceous (80-million-year-old) sandstone rocks in Argentina. These fossil remains are nearly 6 feet (1.8 meters) long and show similarities to some primitive snakes of today. Another famous fossil is the boalike snake remains found in the Geisel Valley, near Halle in Germany. These remains reveal details not only of the snake's skeleton, but also of skin and scales. The largest snake known from fossil remains is an extinct type of python from Middle Eocene rocks in Egypt. Although only partly preserved, this snake may have been as much as 60 feet (18 meters) in length.

Unfortunately, relatively few fossils of snakes have been found in the rocks. To be preserved, an animal must be covered soon after death in mud or sand that later hardens into rock. This is most likely to happen to creatures that sink to the seabed in areas where sediment is being deposited, and so most fossils are of marine creatures. In addition, it is usually only hard parts, such as bones, shells, and teeth, that get preserved. Since snakes lived mostly on land, often in forests, and have only delicate bones, few were preserved as fossils.

Despite the paucity of fossils, there is little doubt that the snakes evolved from lizards with transitional forms appearing in the Cretaceous period. This was the great age of dinosaurs, when reptiles ruled the Earth. It was not until after the dinosaurs had become extinct at the end of the Cretaceous period, about 65 million years ago, that snakes started to diversify significantly and, even today, their evolution is still progressing. In terms of geological time, therefore, the snakes are still a fairly new group, but already there are some 2700 different species, spread all over the world, barring the very cold regions.

Snakes, together with the lizards, and the burrowing amphisbaenids, make up a group known as the *Squamata*. The other groups of living reptiles are the *Crocodilia* (crocodiles and alligators), the *Chelonia* (turtles and tortoises), and the unique *Tuatara* of New Zealand. One of the most obvious features of snakes is their lack of limbs, and this feature is shared by other members of the *Squamata*.

Legless lizards are found all over the world and include the European Glass Lizard (*Ophisaurus apodus*), the California Legless Lizard (*Anniella pulchra*) of North America, and Burton's Snake Lizard (*Lialis burtonis*) of Australia and New Guinea. Other widely distributed lizards, the skinks, show all stages of limb reduction, from normal legs to their total absence. Examples of skinks with tiny legs are the Three-toed Skink (*Chalcides chalcides*) from Europe and the Ground Skink (*Scincella lateralis*) of North America. The amphisbaenids are snakelike members of the *Squamata* that are widely distributed and include the Worm Lizard (*Rhineura floridana*), the only species found in North America. There are about 135 species of these burrowing creatures, and nearly all have lost their limbs during evolution.

The limbless lizards and amphisbaenids are in many other ways dissimilar to snakes and so are not thought to have evolved from the same "legless ancestor." Indeed, the ancestors of the snakes are believed to have had limbs. Instead, the common lack of limbs is thought to be an example of parallel evolution. This occurs when groups of animals independently develop similar adaptations to similar environments or ways of life.

*A Ground Skink* (Scincella lateralis *below left). Some skinks, such as this one, have well-developed limbs, while others have mere vestiges, or are entirely without limbs.*

*The Slender Glass Snake* (Ophisaurus attenuatus *below). This is not a true snake, but a legless lizard found in the U.S.A. A closely related species occurs in eastern Europe. The "glass" in its name comes from the fact that, like other lizards, its tail breaks easily.*

The present-day animal that most closely resembles the ancestors of the snakes is the Earless Monitor (*Lanthanotis borneensis*), a rare type of lizard from Southeast Asia. This animal has all four limbs and, on the surface, looks quite different from snakes. The loss of limbs is thought to have occurred during a burrowing phase in the snake's evolution. It was probably also during this phase that the eyes lost their movable eyelids, reduced in size and became covered by a transparent scale. The senses of smell and taste improved, particularly with the development of Jacobson's organ (see page 28). But the ability to hear airborne sound disappeared with the loss of the external ear opening, the entire middle-ear cavity, tympanic membrane, and the Eustachian tube.

Together with the limbs have gone the shoulder blades, collarbones, breastbones and, in most snakes, the pelvic girdle. Only some of the primitive burrowing snakes and the boas and pythons, whose ancestors date back to the Cretaceous period, have vestigial hind limbs. The skull and the jaws of most snakes have been modified so that they can swallow their prey whole, the latter often being huge in comparison to the size of the snake.

The evolution of venom is relatively recent. During the course of evolution, the saliva glands of poisonous snakes became poison sacs, and teeth developed into fangs for the injection of poison. In some snakes, the fangs have become grooved for the poison to run down. In the most advanced snakes, such as the vipers and cobras, the fangs have developed into tubes, so that poison can be injected like a hypodermic needle or sprayed at an intruder. This ability to deliver poison developed independently in several different snake families.

Other examples of parallel evolution are found within the snakes. For example, the Emerald Tree Boa (*Corallus caninus*) from South America and the Green Tree Python (*Chondropython viridis*) from New Guinea and northern Australia are both very similar-looking large, green, arboreal snakes, but they are not closely related. Some unrelated desert

species have independently developed "horns." These can be seen in the Horned Adder (*Bites caudalis*) and the Desert Horned Viper (*Cerastes cerastes*) from Africa, the North American Sidewinder Rattlesnake (*Crotalus cerastes*), and several other species.

The evolution of snakes also produced a large number of differences in form among species. Together, the different species form a distinct and fascinating group within the *Squamata* order, known as the *Serpentes*.

*An Emerald Tree Boa* (Corallus caninus *above*), *and a Green Tree Python* (Chondropython viridis *left*). *Living in similar tropical forest habitats on different continents, these unrelated snakes have evolved nearly identical coloring and patterning.*

# CLASSIFICATION

In this book, each species of snake is given its scientific name on first mention. This is because the common or vernacular name of a snake may vary from country to country, but its scientific name will usually remain the same. The scientific name is made up of the genus or generic name (the first letter of which is capitalized) and the species or specific name. For example, the Rock Rattlesnake is included in the genus *Crotalus* and has the specific name *lepidus*, so its scientific name is *Crotalus lepidus*. Occasionally there is a third name, too, for example, *Crotalus lepidus klauberi*. The last name indicates that this animal belongs to a distinct group within a species, known as a subspecies. Hence, the Banded Rock Rattlesnake (*Crotalus lepidus klauberi*) is a subspecies of the Rock Rattlesnake (*Crotalus lepidus*), occurring in southwestern U.S.A. and Mexico.

The scientific names of animals have been arrived at by grouping or classifying animals. Modern classifications all derive from a system developed by the Swedish naturalist Carolus Linnaeus (also known as Carl von Linné) and published in 1758. Once his system became universally accepted, it was possible to start arranging animals into groups. Our present-day classifications attempt to group animals together to show their relationships with one another and their evolution.

The reptiles are divided into various groups called orders, one of which is the *Squamata*. This, in turn, is divided into three groups: the lizards, snakes, and amphisbaenids. The group of snakes (*Serpentes*) is split up into three infraorders: the *Scolecophidia*, the *Henophidia*, and the *Caenophidia*. Within these infraorders, the 2700 different species of snakes are arranged in families.

## PRIMITIVE BURROWING SNAKES

The *Scolecophidia* consists of three families of snakes that have evolved quite differently from all other snakes. They are highly specialized for life under the ground, and the size of the mouth has been drastically reduced.

The family *Leptotyphlopidae*, or thread snakes, contains about 50 species, which live in arid areas of Africa, Asia, and North and South America. All are less than 16 inches (40 centimeters) in length, and are very slender and wormlike, with overlapping, highly polished scales. They have teeth only on the lower jaw, and have a vestigial pelvic girdle and hind limbs. They have only one lung and a single oviduct. They feed on small invertebrates such as ants, termites, and insect larvae.

The family *Typhlopidae*, or blind snakes, are similar to the thread snakes, but have teeth on the upper jaw only. They also have a lung that extends forward and surrounds the windpipe (a tracheal lung) and lack an enlarged scale in front of the anus. There are about 180 species distributed over many of the warmer parts of the world, and they eat small invertebrates, especially ants.

The third family of burrowing snakes, the *Anomalepididae*, superficially resemble the thread and blind snakes, but lack even a vestigial pelvic girdle and have teeth on both upper and lower jaws. There are about 20 species, confined to tropical South America.

**SNAKES AND LIZARDS**
Closely related to snakes, lizards show a wide range of limb structure from being fully limbed (5) to the completely limbless glass lizards (2) of Europe and North America. Some species have only front limbs, while others have all limbs very much reduced (3), or almost absent (1). The worm lizards (4) are usually placed in a separate group, distinct from both snakes and lizards. Although fully limbed, the Earless Monitor (5) is the living lizard believed to be most closely related to snakes.

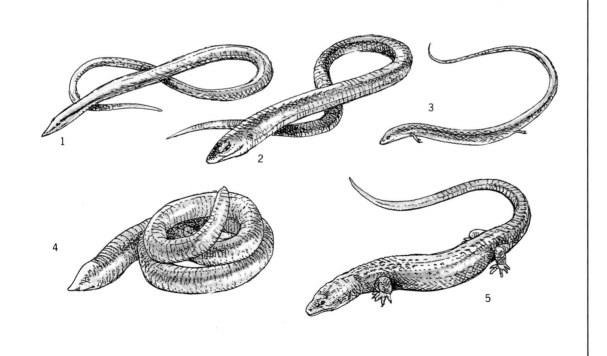

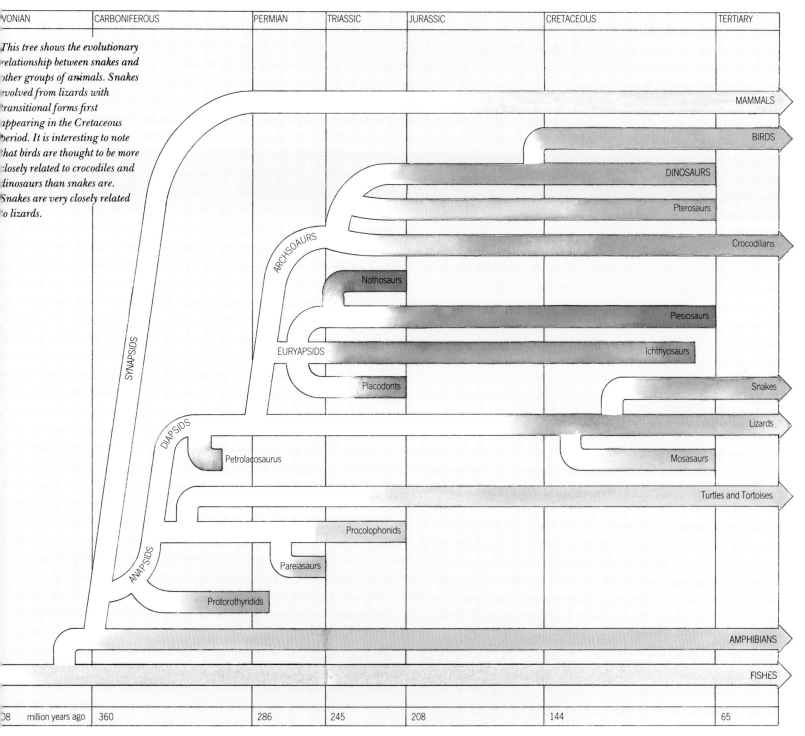

This tree shows the evolutionary relationship between snakes and other groups of animals. Snakes evolved from lizards with transitional forms first appearing in the Cretaceous period. It is interesting to note that birds are thought to be more closely related to crocodiles and dinosaurs than snakes are. Snakes are very closely related to lizards.

## BOAS AND THEIR RELATIVES

The *Henophidia* consists of five families. The family *Aniliidae*, or pipe snakes, contains a single South American species (*Anilis scytale*) and about nine species from Southeast Asia. All have vestigial hind limbs and enlarged plates or scales on their belly or ventral side. The mouth is not very flexible and so they cannot eat large prey. They are all burrowing snakes and hunt slender snakes, caecilians (burrowing legless amphibians) and amphisbaenids.

Within the family *Uropeltidae,* or shield-tailed, snakes are about 40 species, all burrowers, living in hilly and mountainous areas of southern India and Sri Lanka. Each has a short tail, terminating in a single, large, rough scale which may possess one or more spines. They have narrow, pointed heads on very flexible necks, and all their scales are highly polished, the ventral ones being small.

The family *Xenopeltidae* consists of just one little-known species, the Sunbeam Snake (*Xenopeltis unicolor*) from Southeast Asia. Its most outstanding feature is the iridescence of its shiny, smooth scales. It has two lungs, large ventral scales, and a rigid skull.

By far the best-known family within this group is the *Boidae*. It comprises some 95 species of boas and pythons occurring in a wide range of habitats, and includes the largest snakes in the world. Boids are an ancient group of snakes, with fossil ancestors having been found in rocks of Cretaceous age. As a result of this long history, the boids have evolved into many widely differing forms. So the family is often divided into subfamilies: the *Boinae* (boas), the *Erycinae* (sand boas, Rosy Boa and Rubber Boa), the *Bolyerinae* (Round Island boas), the *Loxocerimae* (Mexican Dwarf Boa), the *Trophidophinae* (dwarf boas), the *Calabarinae* (Calabar Ground Python), and the *Pythoninae* (pythons). The main characteristics of the family are the presence of vestigial hind limbs and pelvic girdle, and the flexible jaws, not found in more primitive snakes. All have a right lung and some may also have a left lung, a primitive feature found otherwise only in the Sunbeam Snake.

The final family within this group is the *Acrochordidae*, or wart snakes. There are only three species, found in Southeast Asia, from Indonesia to Papua New Guinea and northern Australia, where they live in coastal and estuarine waters. Their aquatic way of life, granular-scaled skin, lack of vestigial hind limbs and pelvis, single lung, and flexible skull are the main characteristics of the group.

## VIPERS, COBRAS, GRASS SNAKES AND THEIR RELATIVES

The *Caenophidia* contains the majority of the world's snakes, within the three families, the *Colubridae*, the *Elapidae* and the *Viperidae*. By far the largest of these is the *Colubridae*, which contains over 2000 species – more than all the other groups put together. They are distributed throughout the world and are dominant everywhere, except Australia. The *Colubridae* is divided into eight subfamilies, and over half the world's snakes are in two of these, the *Colubrinae* and *Natricinae*.

Snakes in the *Colubrinae* and *Nactricinae* are found in both the Old and New Worlds and show many adaptations to the vast range of climates and environments in which they live. Many members of the *Nactricinae* are associated with water. Although most species in these subfamilies are nonvenomous, some are venomous, and a few of these, such as the Boomslang (*Dispholidus typus*) and the Twig Snake (*Thelotornis kirtlandi*), are dangerous to people. All of the venomous forms are backfanged.

Of the other six subfamilies, the *Xenodermatinae* contains species from Southeast Asia, which are similar to the wart snakes. The 16 species belonging to the *Pareinae* are slug-eating snakes from Asia. The *Dipsadinae* comprises about 60 species from South America, all of which specialize in eating land snails. The six African and one Asian species in the *Dasypeltinae* are all egg-eating snakes. Within the *Homalopsinae* are about 35 species of backfanged water snakes. Among the *Aparallactinae*'s 60 species of African and Middle Eastern burrowing snakes are the mole vipers.

The *Elapidae* comprises about 169 species, which are usually divided into three subfamilies: the *Elapinae*, the *Hydrophinae* and the *Laticaudinae*. The *Elapinae* are all terrestrial and include the cobras, coral snakes, mambas and kraits. They are found in both the Old and New World, although very few occur in temperate parts of the northern hemisphere. Fossils of cobras have been found in France, but they no longer occur anywhere in Europe.

The sea snakes, *Hydrophinae* and *Laticaudinae*, are among the most completely aquatic of all airbreathing vertebrates. With the exception of a few freshwater species, they are almost completely marine. They range throughout most of the tropical parts of the Pacific Ocean, the Indonesian archipelago to northern Australia, and the Indian Ocean as

*The skin of the Wart Snake (*Acrochordus granulatus *right). While the body of most snakes is covered in overlapping scales, with platelike scales on the head, this aquatic species has a granular skin.*

far as the Cape of Good Hope. The 35 species of *Hydrophinae* all feed on fish and give birth to live young. They are not aggressive but have been known to bite people on the odd occasion, particularly fishermen, and, as their venom is highly toxic, they do cause fatalities. Some of the 11 species in the *Laticaudinae* come ashore to lay their eggs, while others give birth to live young.

In the *Viperidae*, the roughly 182 species are divided among three subfamilies: the *Azemiopinae*, the *Viperinae* and the *Crotalinae*. The *Azemiopinae* consists of a single primitive species from the mountains of southern China, Tibet and Burma.

The *Viperinae*, or true vipers, are restricted to the Old World, where they have colonized a wide variety of habitats. They comprise about 60 species, all of which are venomous, including some that are dangerous to people.

Among the *Crotalinae*, or pit vipers, one genus is restricted to Asia, another occurs in both Asia and America, but most are found only in the New World, including the rattlesnakes. The pit vipers differ from the true vipers in having a heat-sensitive pit between the nostril and the eye. They are all venomous, but not all are dangerous to people.

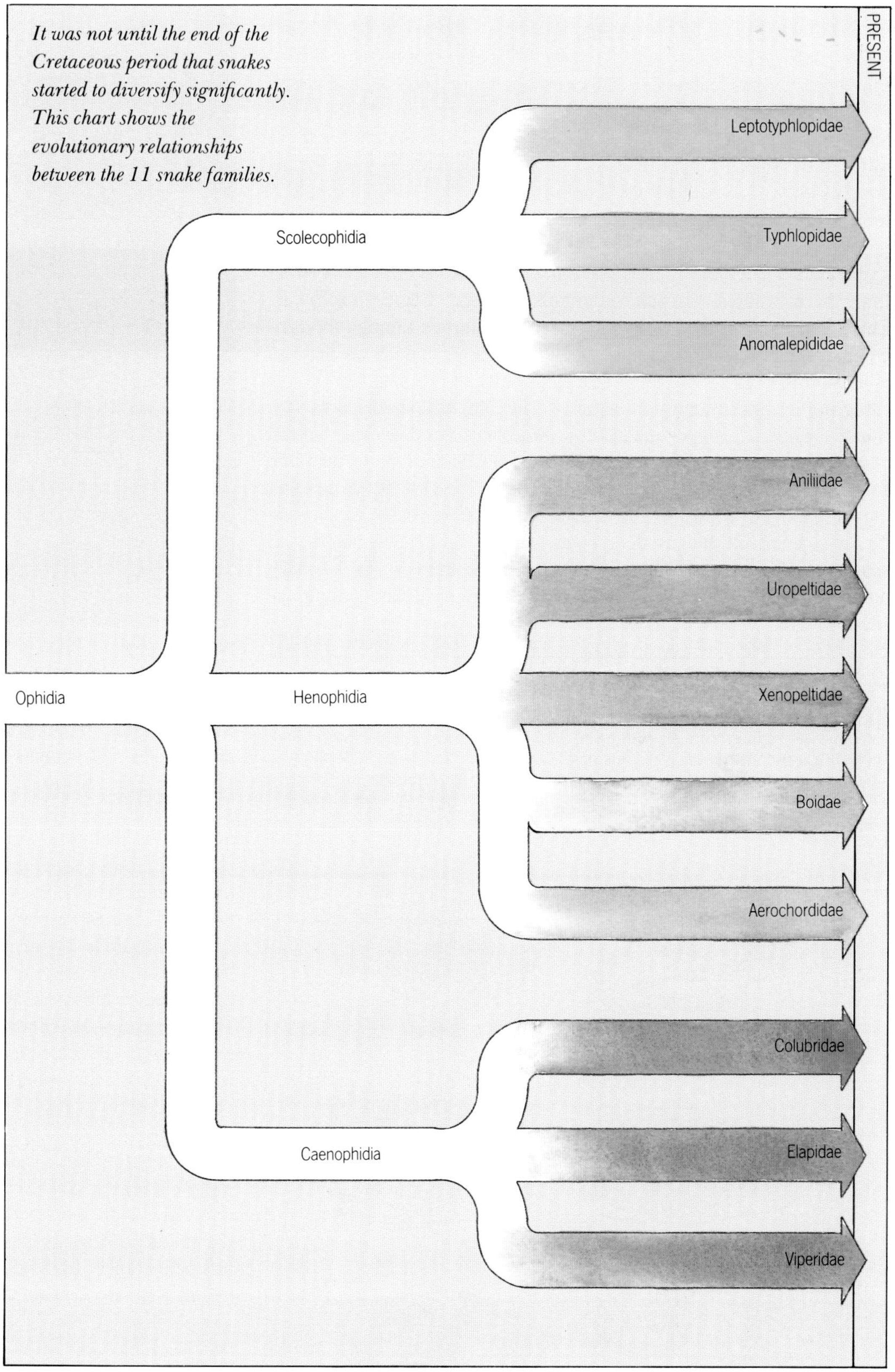

*It was not until the end of the Cretaceous period that snakes started to diversify significantly. This chart shows the evolutionary relationships between the 11 snake families.*

*It was not until the end of the Cretaceous period that snakes started to diversify significantly. This chart shows the evolutionary relationships between the 11 snake families.*

PRESENT

Scolecophidia

Leptotyphlopidae

Typhlopidae

Anomalepididae

Aniliidae

Uropeltidae

Xenopeltidae

Boidae

Aerochordidae

Colubridae

Elapidae

Viperidae

Ophidia

Henophidia

Caenophidia

# THE SNAKE'S BODY

The most obvious features of snakes are their elongated body and lack of limbs. Primitive snakes often have remnants of pelvic girdles and hind limbs. These can be seen as tiny spurs or cloacal claws and are relics of the snakes's lizardlike ancestors. The skeleton of most snakes consists only of a skull, a long vertebral column, and ribs. The spine is fairly uniform along the whole of its length and contains between 150–450 vertebrae, each with a pair of ribs. The vertebrae are linked by ball and socket joints, and by winglike projections or processes that limit the movement of each vertebra to about 25 degrees each way. This prevents damage to the spinal cord, which runs through the center of the backbone, and protects the blood vessels and nerves that run alongside it.

In primitive snakes, the skull is fairly rigid, but most snakes have very flexible skulls. The upper and lower jaws are loosely connected, and can come apart from each other and from the braincase or cranium, enabling snakes to swallow prey much larger than themselves. The teeth are often curved strongly backward, and in most poisonous species one pair, the fangs, is enlarged and used to inject venom. While the majority of snakes have teeth in both lower and upper jaws, the worm snakes have teeth only in the upper jaw, and the thread snakes have them only in the lower jaw.

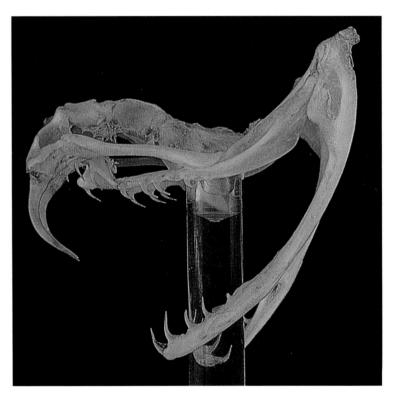

*The skull of a Western Diamondback Rattlesnake (Crotalus atrox) (above), showing the massive hollow fangs, characteristic of pit vipers and vipers, which swing down to inject venom. If the fangs are broken, a replacement set will grow.*

## SNAKE SKULLS

A Sunbeam Snake **(1)** with the shovel-shaped snout of a burrowing snake. The Boa Constrictor **(2)** and the Bull Snake **(3)** both have relatively uniform teeth. A poisonous member of the *Colubridae* family, *Tomodon dorsatus* **(4)**, has poison fangs set well back on the upper jaw. The Death Adder **(5)** has the reduced dentition typical of elapids, and two large fangs at the front of the jaw. The massive fangs of the Temple Pit Viper **(6)** swing sideways when the jaw is shut, and behind them, replacement fangs are growing.

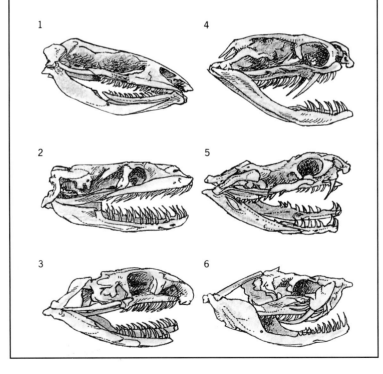

## MUSCLES

Snake musculature is very complicated, consisting of many different individual muscles and muscle cords. It is the coordinated interaction of the muscles which gives snakes their smooth, gliding motion. Three pairs of long muscle cords run along the backbone, connecting the vertebrae, and these are responsible for the smooth curving of the body. There are numerous muscles on the vertebral processes, which, when contracted, bring about the tight curves or loops in the snake's body. They have muscles connecting ribs together, and vertebrae to ribs. The skin muscles, which connect scales to scales and scales to ribs, are also important in locomotion.

## ORGANS

The elongation of the snake's body has affected the shape and positioning of its organs. Snakes usually have only a single functional lung, the right one, with the left lung absent or considerably reduced in size. Exceptions are some boas and the Sunbeam Snake, which have both lungs functional. In the majority of snakes, the single lung is elongated.

Both male and female reproductive organs have been modified by the snake's shape. The male's penis is divided into two hemipenis, which are very variable and often covered with distinctive backward-pointing spines. The testes are staggered, with the right one farther forward. The female's ovaries may be similarly placed, or the left oviduct may be absent altogether.

## INTERNAL ANATOMY
Because of their elongated body, the organs inside a snake are stretched out and usually asymmetrical.

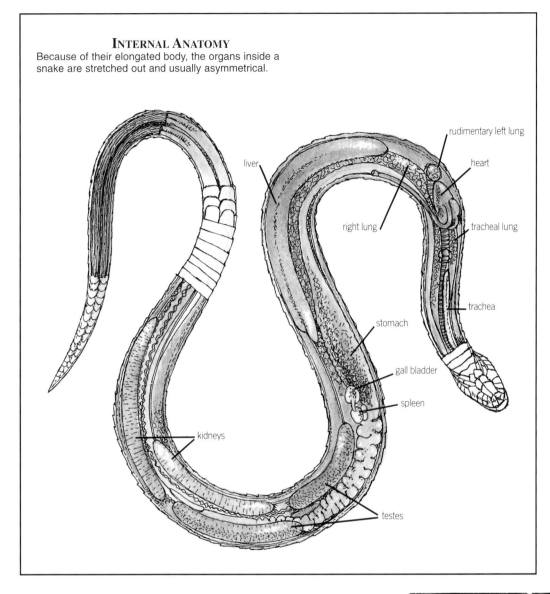

liver

rudimentary left lung

heart

right lung

tracheal lung

trachea

stomach

gall bladder

spleen

kidneys

testes

is very elastic, and the scales stretch apart when the snake is swallowing and digesting large prey.

## TYPES OF SCALES
In each species of snake, the number and arrangement of the scales is fairly constant and so scales are an important aid to identification. The scales on the head are typically large, but may be small, such as in boas and vipers. The body is normally covered with small scales on the upper or dorsal side. The dorsal scales vary in texture and may be smooth, keeled, or granular, depending on the species, but are most commonly glossy and overlapping. There are usually large platelike scales on the belly or ventral side, but these are not present in primitive snakes, and in the boas and pythons they are relatively small. The underside of the tail has single or paired scales.

*A Milk Snake* (Lampropeltis triangulum *below) from the high plains of Texas.*

The digestive system of snakes is modified in various ways. The stomach is merely a slight widening of the alimentary canal, and the intestines are only slightly coiled toward the end. The elongated liver is situated alongside the lung, and the gall bladder is just below the stomach, opening into the small intestine, rather than within the liver. The kidneys are not "kidney-shaped," but are elongated and staggered, with the left positioned behind the right. Snakes lack a bladder and do not excrete urine. Instead, waste nitrogenous matter is excreted as uric acid crystals with the feces.

## SNAKESKIN
The skin of most snakes is impermeable to water, which prevents dehydration and is a vital factor in enabling them to live in arid desert regions. The dry skin is made up of three layers. The inner layer is the thickest and contains the pigment cells, the middle layer is very thin and consists of growing and dividing cells, and the tough outer layer comprises various types of plates or scales made up of dead cells. The skin

A closeup (left) of the head and skin of a Javan File Snake (Acrochordus javanicus).

A racer (Coluber constrictor oppisite above) beginning to shed its skin. Just prior to molting, the snake's coloring becomes milky and dull. The sloughing process starts at the mouth and continues backward, often leaving behind a perfect skin turned inside out. The snake sheds its entire skin, including the covering of its eyes.

## SKIN-SHEDDING

All snakes have to shed or slough the hard outer coating of their skin periodically in order to grow. When the old skin is due to be shed, fluid is produced between the old and the new skin, causing the snake's coloring to become dull and milky. The actual sloughing is started by the snake rubbing its head against objects. The skin is usually shed in one piece, from the head and continuing down the whole of the body, turning inside out in the process. The time between skin-shedding varies; younger snakes shed their skin more often than older ones.

## COLOR

Most terrestrial snakes are brown or gray and so are well camouflaged. Similarly, arboreal snakes which live in foliage tend to be green. Desert species are often yellow or red, depending on the type of sand present. The patterning on some snakes disrupts their outline; this is particularly well developed in some of the vipers, notably the Gaboon Viper (*Bitis gabonica*), and in rattlesnakes. Another example is the Boa Constrictor, which harmonizes well with its jungle background and has stripes that obscure outlines of head and eye.

A snake's color and pattern is caused by pigmentation, or the lack of it, and the physical nature of the surface of the scales. The surface structure

The rattle on the tail of a Western Diamondback Rattlesnake (Crotalus atrox *above*). The age of these snakes cannot be told accurately from the number of rattles.

## THE RATTLE

A modification to the scales found in rattlesnakes is a series of bony interlocking rings at the end of the tail which form the rattle. A young rattlesnake is born with a single knob or button, and a new segment is added every time it sheds its skin. Rattles of more than 10 segments are rare, however, as segments of the rattle gradually break off. When disturbed, the snake vibrates the rattle, producing a loud buzz, with the speed of the vibration depending on the snake's degree of excitement.

The end scale of the tail thickens before the second molt.

After the second molt, a new scale grows on the tip inside the old one.

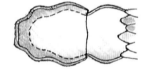

Before the next molt, the tip of the second scale shrinks.

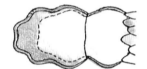

After the next molt, a third scale grows inside the second.

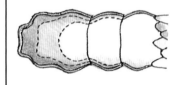

*The overlapping scales (left) of a Reticulated Python (Python reticulatus).*

*The harmless Milk Snake (Lampropeltis triangulum top left) mimics the warning coloration of the highly poisonous coral snakes.*

*The contrasting bright colors of this coral snake (Micrurus fulvius bottom left) warn would-be predators that the snake is very poisonous.*

*The tiny Redbelly Snake (Storeria occipitomuculata, below right) of eastern North America is among the smallest snakes known, being less than 8 inches (20 centimeters) long when it reaches maturity.*

can give the scales an iridescence, as in the Sunbeam Snake and the Rainbow Boa (*Epicrates cenchria*). Where all pigments except yellow are absent, a totally yellow snake is produced. Where melanin (dark brown or black pigment) is predominant, a melanic or dark snake occurs. There are increasing numbers of melanic individuals within many species, such as some vipers. Melanic snakes commonly do well in the wild because their dark coloring allows them to absorb heat more readily. Albinism, caused by a total lack of skin pigments, is less common, since in the wild albino snakes easily fall prey to their enemies.

Snakes also show other variations in colors and markings within a single species. The young of the Green Tree Python may be red, yellow, or brown. The King Snake (*Lampropeltis getulus*) from North America has seven subspecies, all with different coloring, ranging from pure black or black with light crossbands to a chainlike pattern on either a brown or black background.

## SIZE

The length of snakes varies enormously, from a few inches to nearly 30 feet (9 meters). It is actually quite difficult to measure accurately the length of a live snake, because its body is usually curved and it is difficult to handle. Dead snakes also present difficulties when they are being measured, because they are easily stretched beyond their normal length, as are snakes' discarded skins. So measurements of snakes have to be carefully taken and checked.

## MIMICRY

Coral snakes and *Lampropeltis* species are so similar to each other that it has been suggested that both mimic a third, less poisonous group of similarly colored snakes, such as species of *Erythrolamprus*. Predators attacking the latter would only suffer mild poisoning, but this would be enough to deter them from attacking brightly colored snakes again. Thus, the very poisonous and nonpoisonous mimics would also gain protection. The flaw in this theory is that while all three groups occur in South America, the two mimics also occur in North America without the mildly poisonous "model" to mimic.

## SIZE RECORDS

Currently, the honor of being the largest snake is shared by two species – the Reticulated Python (*Python reticulatus*) from Southeast Asia and the Anaconda (*Eunectes murinus*) from South America. Specimens of both have been reliably measured at more than 29½ feet (9 meters). There have been reports of 33-foot (10-meter) or more specimens, including an Anaconda reputed to be 62 feet (18.89 meters) long, but these have not been verified. It is quite feasible that a 33-foot (10-meter) Anaconda could exist in remote and unexplored parts of its range. However, in the 1940s, the New York Zoological Society offered a reward of $5000 for a living specimen of any snake over 30 feet (9.14 meters) long, and the money has never been claimed.

Most of the longest species are boas or pythons, all of which are nonpoisonous. They include the African Python (*Python sebae*), which may grow up to 29½ feet (9 meters); the Indian Python up to 21 feet (6.5 meters), and the Boa Constrictor, up to 20 feet (6 meters). The King Cobra is the largest poisonous snake, growing up to 18⅓ feet (5.6 meters), followed by the Black Mamba (*Dendroaspis polylepis*) at 14 feet (4.3 meters), and the Taipan (*Oxyuranus scutellatus*) at 14 feet (4.3 meters). The longest snakes in North America include the Indigo Snake (*Drymarchon corais*) and the Coachwhip (*Masticophis flagellum*), both of which reach 8½ feet (2.6 meters). In Europe, the Large Whip Snake (*Coluber jugularis*) and the Four-lined Snake (*Elaphe quatuorlineata*) both reach 8¼ feet (2.5 meters). The vast majority of snakes fall within the range 1½-6½ feet (0.45-2.0 meters) in length.

By far the heaviest snake is the Anaconda, which is much bulkier than the Reticulated Python. A 26-foot (8-meter) Anaconda was found to weigh nearly 400 pounds (180 kilograms), whereas a Reticulated Python of similar length weighed only 250 pounds (115 kilograms).

Some much shorter snakes are very stoutly built and heavy for their size. This is particularly true of some of the pythons, notably the Malaysian Short Python (*Python curtus*), and the Puff Adder (*Bitis arietans*) from Africa. At the other end of the scale, some tree snakes can be quite long and extremely thin. One of the longest and most slender is the Tree Snake (*Imantodes cenchoa*), and other examples include the Twig Snake and the Long-nosed Tree Snake (*Dryophis nasuta*).

The smallest are worm snakes and thread snakes. A worm snake, the Brahminy Blind Snake (*Ramphotyphlops braminus*), is usually less than 6 inches (15 centimeters) long, and the thread snakes of the genus *Leptotyphlops* are only some 3-4 inches (8-10 centimeters) in length.

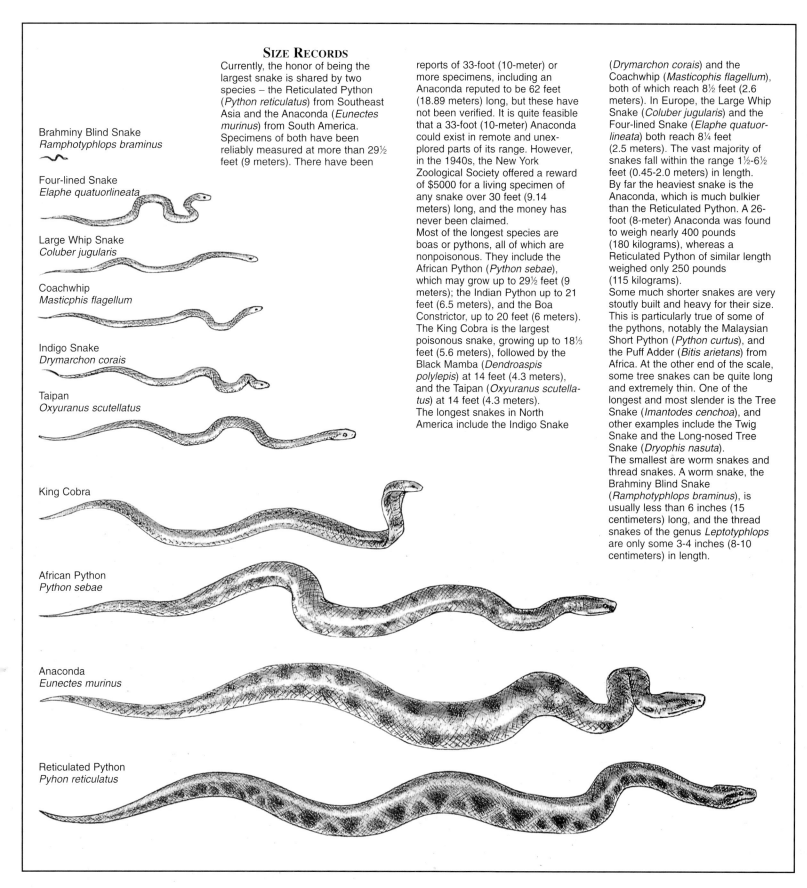

Brahminy Blind Snake
*Ramphotyphlops braminus*

Four-lined Snake
*Elaphe quatuorlineata*

Large Whip Snake
*Coluber jugularis*

Coachwhip
*Masticphis flagellum*

Indigo Snake
*Drymarchon corais*

Taipan
*Oxyuranus scutellatus*

King Cobra

African Python
*Python sebae*

Anaconda
*Eunectes murinus*

Reticulated Python
*Pyhon reticulatus*

# MOVEMENT

Although we usually say that snakes "crawl," they can actually move in four different ways – serpentine movement, concertina movement, rectilinear creeping, and sidewinding. The type of movement used depends largely on the terrain.

In serpentine movement, the snake's body is bent into horizontal loops by the contraction of muscles on the inner side of each loop. As the contractions move along the snake, a series of waves passes from the head backward. On land, serpentine movement is only possible where there are irregularities in the ground for the waves to push against, propelling the snake forward. Snakes also use this movement when swimming, with the water taking the place of irregularities in propelling the snake forward.

Concertina movement is used when crawling over difficult terrain or in a confined space, such as a burrow. The snake wedges the back part of the body and extends the rest of the body forward as far as possible. It then wedges the head and "concertinas" the front of the body, drawing itself forward. The snake then wedges the back part again and repeats the process.

Rectilinear creeping is used particularly by large and heavy snakes, such as boas and pythons, and allows them to move in a straight line. The snake uses the muscles joining the ventral scales to the ribs, contracting them in waves down the body. The ventral scales grip onto irregularities in the ground, and the snake is propelled forward in a seemingly effortless gliding motion.

Sidewinding relies least on a firm surface to push against and is used by snakes living in areas with shifting surfaces, such as desert sands. Snakes employing this method include the Sidewinder Rattlesnake, Peringuey's Desert Adder (*Bitis peringueyi*), and McMahon's Viper (*Eristicophis macmahoni*). In sidewinding, the snake shifts itself by moving sideways in a series of steps at an angle of about 45 degrees to the line of the body. The snake lifts its head off the ground and thrusts it to the side. As the head touches the ground, the body follows it, lifted across by a loop that travels down to the tail using the vertical pressure at the point of contact to prevent the snake from slipping. The head is then lifted and moved sideways again. The track left is a series of parallel lines in the sand where the snake was in contact with the ground.

Some snakes have developed other forms of movement. Sea snakes, for example, commonly have a flattened tail which they use as a paddle. The

## SNAKE LOCOMOTION

Snakes have evolved several different ways of moving, and may vary their method of locomotion depending on the terrain.

**1** Rectilinear movement. In this form of locomotion, the snake literally creeps along on its belly, using waves of muscular contractions along the length of the body.

**2** Serpentine movement. In this most common form of locomotion, the snake levers its body against stones, vegetation, and even the flat ground. Some snakes use this motion so effectively that they can propel themselves up to a yard into the air.

**3** Concertina movement. This is generally used when the snake is in a confined space, such as a rodent burrow or rock cleft. It wedges the back of the body and extends forward, then wedges the front of the body and draws the rear up.

**4** Sidewinding. This spectacular form of movement enables a snake to move rapidly across loose sand and smooth surfaces. The snake progresses diagonally in a series of loops, relying on the vertical pressure where the body makes contact with the ground to prevent sliding.

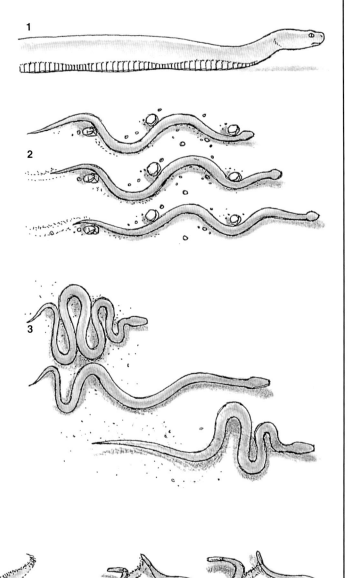

Jumping Viper (*Bothrops mummifer*) from South America can hurl itself for a yard or more to catch prey. The so-called flying snakes, such as the Golden Tree Snake (*Chrysopelea ornata*) from Southeast Asia, launch themselves from high trees and glide by extending the belly sideways so that it becomes concave and can act like a parachute.

In the past many exaggerated claims were made about the speeds that snakes can attain. In fact, however they move, the majority are rather slow. For example, some North American whip snakes and racers (*Masticophis* and *Coluber*) were said to move at 15 mph (24 km/h). Speed tests carried out on several of these snakes in the 1930s showed that the fastest are the Red Coachwhip (*Masticophis flagellum piceus*) at 3.5 mph (5.7 km/h) and the Black Racer (*Coluber constrictor constrictor*) at 3.6 mph (5.9 km/h). The European Grass Snake (*Natrix natrix*) is relatively fast at 4.2 mph (6.7 km/h).

The fastest snake in the world is almost certainly the Black Mamba. Speeds of up to 20 mph (32 km/h) have been claimed for this species, but a top speed of 10 mph (16 km/h) over short distances is probably more accurate. The fastest swimming snakes are the sea snakes of the Indo-Pacific region. It is possible that some, such as the Yellow-bellied Sea Snake (*Pelamis platurus*) reach a speed of 10 mph (16 km/h) over short distances when pursuing prey.

*The characteristic tracks (right) left by Peringuey's Desert Adder (Bitis peringueyi) sidewinding in the sands of the Namib Desert. Sidewinding is a form of locomotion used by snakes to move across very smooth surfaces or loose, shifting surfaces such as desert sands.*

# THE SENSES

Snakes gather information about the world in a very different way from us. While we rely mainly on sight and hearing, these senses are relatively poorly developed in snakes. Instead, they depend on other stimuli, particularly scents and, in some cases, heat.

Snakes are often said to be deaf because they lack outer ears and Eustachian tubes, and are, therefore, unable to receive airborne sound waves. However, they do have an inner ear which reacts acutely to ground vibrations. To detect these, the lower jaw must be in contact with the ground. The vibrations are then transmitted via bones, and possibly also the lung, to the ear.

The eyes of snakes vary between species, but are usually rather inefficient, snakes having evolved from burrowing animals that had little need of sight. They are unable to change the shape of the lens in the eye to focus, and most have no movable eyelids, giving them a large, staring, unblinking gaze. Those active in the day usually have rounded pupils, while nocturnal species, such as boas, pythons, vipers, and pit vipers, generally have vertical slit pupils. The slit reduces the amount of light falling on the eye's light-sensitive cells during the day. The Long-nosed Tree Snake has a horizontal pupil and grooves running down its pointed snout from the eyes, allowing it some degree of binocular vision.

Of all the senses, that of smell is probably the most important to snakes. Prey, predators, and members of the opposite sex are all revealed by the scent chemicals they emit. The nose plays little part in detecting these scents. Instead, the snake smells – or perhaps, more accurately, tastes – the scents using an organ known as Jacobson's organ, situated on the palate. Scent particles from the air are picked up by the snake's forked tongue which constantly darts in and out of the mouth through a notch in the lip. The tongue transfers the scent to the sacklike Jacobson's organ, lined with scent-sensitive cells, and this transfers the information to the brain.

The tongue is also used in the sense of touch, as are small tubercles, especially on the snout and chin, and sometimes on the belly and tail. In addition, there are sometimes areas of thinning on the scales, known as apical pits, and the epidermis under these is particularly rich in nerve fibers. It is possible these apical pits may be heat receptors.

All snakes are sensitive to temperature changes in their environment and to infrared radiation. Some boas and pythons, and all pit vipers, have developed this sensitivity into a powerful tool for detecting warm-blooded prey. They have special heat receptors or sensory pits situated on each side of the head, between the eye and the nostril. These are acutely sensitive to the most minute temperature changes in their surroundings, those of pit vipers being able to sense temperature changes of as little as 0.005 degrees Fahrenheit (0.003 degrees Centigrade.) With the aid of the pits, the snake can detect and accurately strike at warm-blooded prey, even in total darkness.

*The Trans-Pecos Rat Snake (Elaphe subocularis, right) photographed in the Big Bend region of Texas. The round pupil is characteristic of diurnal snakes, although this species often becomes nocturnal during the heat of summer.*

## EYES

All snakes lack lids to the eyes, but otherwise the form of the eyes is very variable. Diurnal snakes **(1)** usually have circular pupils. Some nocturnal snakes **(2)** have vertical, slitlike pupils. Burrowing snakes **(3)** often have an almost opaque scale completely covering each eye. Tree snakes **(4)** have some of the most interesting adaptations – the horizontal pupils, bulbous protruding eyes, and a grooved and tapering snout, which together give them binocular vision.

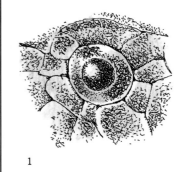

1

2

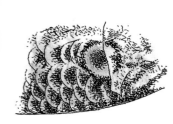

3

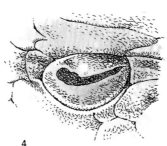

4

The vertical pupil (above left) of the Boa Constrictor is characteristic of nocturnal snakes. During daylight, the pupil contacts to a narrow slit and then widens at night.

The head of the Sidelined Tree Viper (Bothrops Lateralis) (above left). The heat-sensitive pits in front of the eyes of this pit viper can be clearly seen.

A Northern Copperhead (Agkistrodon contortrix) with its tongue extruded (left). This organ is "tasting" the air and cannot be used to sting as is popularly believed. The tongue picks up particles and then transfers them to the mouth.

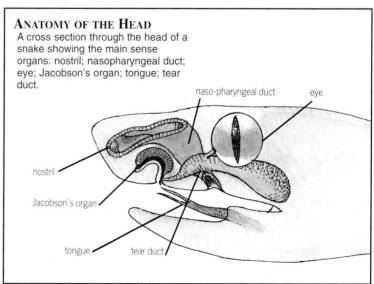

**ANATOMY OF THE HEAD**
A cross section through the head of a snake showing the main sense organs: nostril; nasopharyngeal duct; eye; Jacobson's organ; tongue; tear duct.

# TEMPERATURE CONTROL

Although not strictly "cold-blooded," as is generally believed, reptiles generate much less heat than mammals and birds. With no insulating layer of blubber, fur, hair, or feathers, they also lose heat far more rapidly. As a snake cools, it becomes less and less active, and below 35–39 degrees Fahrenheit (2–4 degrees Centigrade), it becomes completely torpid and may die.

Snakes rely on the heat of the sun to raise their temperature and allow them to move freely. However, they then run the risk of becoming too hot, because they lack sweat glands and so are unable to reduce their body temperature by perspiration. And if their temperature rises above 100–117 degrees Fahrenheit (38–47 degrees Centigrade) for any length of time, snakes die. So they move between sun and shade and use other techniques to try to keep their body at the optimum temperature, which varies from species to species. For example, the nocturnal (night-active) Sidewinder Rattlesnake has a preferred temperature of 90 degrees Fahrenheit (32 degrees Centigrade) and that of the diurnal (day-active) Coachwhip is 79 degrees Fahrenheit (26 degrees Centigrade), although both species may share the same desert habitat.

Despite these temperature restrictions, some 2700 species of snake have colonized most of the world, except the very coldest regions. Tropical areas offer the most stable temperature environment and so are home to the most species of snakes and support the greatest number per unit area. There, nocturnal or burrowing snakes are able to remain active all year round. Diurnal snakes, though, may need to estivate (remain inactive) during the hottest months of the year, or may become active only at twilight. Other adaptations to hot environments include pale coloration to reflect heat. The largest species in the world are found in tropical areas, such as the Anaconda and the Reticulated Python. Conversely, the snakes found in colder regions and at higher altitudes often have a dark coloration, which absorbs more heat, and are smaller, so having less mass to heat up. In these regions, the temperature is often too low for snakes to remain active during winter, and

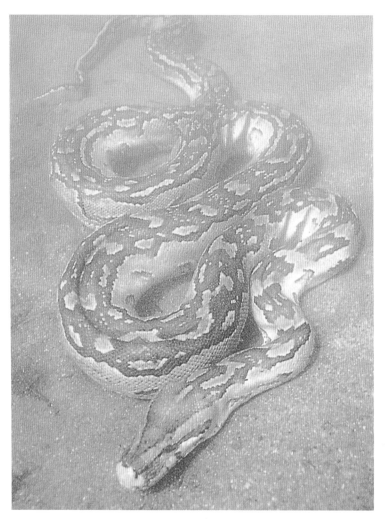

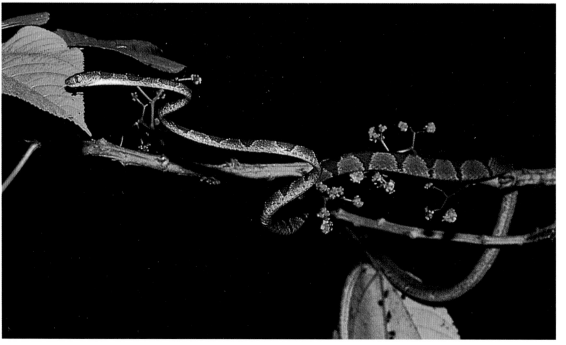

*Larger snakes, such as pythons and boas, frequently enter water to cool down (top). A widespread species in Africa, the African Python (Python sebae) often rests or even hunts in water.*

*The Blunt-headed Tree Snake (Imantodes cenchoa) (left) is a very long, slender, arboreal and nocturnal snake.*

to survive, they must hibernate in frostfree underground refuges. The length of hibernation depends solely on the length of the cold weather which, in the case of the Adder (*Vipera berus*), varies from 105 days in southern Europe to 275 days in the far north. No snake can survive where the subsoil is permanently frozen, as in the polar regions. The Adder is found farther north than any other snake, crossing the Arctic Circle, and reaching a latitude of 68 degrees north in Scandinavia. The Common Garter Snake (*Thamnophis sirtalis*) from North America reaches a latitude of 67 degrees north in the Yukon, hibernating in community dens in vast numbers in the northern part of its range. The most southerly snake in the world is a pit viper (*Bothrops ammodytoides*), which has been found in the region around Santa Cruz in Argentina.

There are, perhaps surprisingly, quite a large number of snakes that inhabit mountainous areas, although only relatively few are found at altitudes of over 10,000 feet (3000 meters). In Europe, the Adder occurs up to 10,000 feet (3000 meters) in the Swiss Alps. In North America, the Western Terrestrial Garter Snake (*Thamnophis elegans*) is found at up to 10,500 feet (3200 meters) and the Western Rattlesnake (*Crotalus viridis*) at up to 10,990 feet (3350 meters). The altitude record is held by the Himalayan Pit Viper (*Agkistrodon himalayanus*), found up to 16,000 feet (4900 meters) in the Himalayas.

As the temperature changes throughout the year, snakes may change their habits accordingly. In areas where it is only hot in the middle of the day, in spring and fall, snakes have to bask in the midday sun to increase their body temperature to the required level. The Adder, often active at twilight or night in the southern part of its range, adapts to the colder northern areas by becoming diurnal.

*The Common Garter Snake (Thamnophis sirtalis) (above right) occurs farther north than any other snake in the New World. In the northern parts of its range, it often congregates in huge numbers when hibernating.*

*Adders (Vipera berus) (above left) basking in the sun. Most snakes do this in order to raise their body temperature to the optimum for activity.*

# LIFE CYCLE

A new snake's life begins when a male and female mate, resulting in the fertilization of the female's eggs by the male. The embryo snakes develop inside the mother and then may be laid in eggs and incubated or be born live. The young feed, shedding their skin periodically as they grow. If they avoid becoming food for other predators, they will reach sexual maturity and complete their life cycle.

### MALES AND FEMALES

As far as is known, there are males and females of all species of snake but one. The exception is the Brahminy Blind Snake, widely distributed throughout the warmer parts of the world and only occurring as a female. With no males to mate with, the females produce offspring from unfertilized eggs, known as parthenogenesis, and all the young are females.

Among other snakes; there are usually few external differences between the sexes. Females may be heavier and longer than males, and have a relatively shorter tail. In the boas and pythons, the "claws" (vestiges of hind limbs) are two or three times larger in males than females. The coloration is usually similar, but, for example, in the Adder, the males are silvery gray with black zigzag markings, and the females are usually brownish or reddish-brown with dark-brown markings.

The male's penis is divided into two organs, each known as a hemipenis. These normally lie inside out within the male snake, at the base of the tail. The hemipenis is a complex structure and often has backward-pointing spines to hold itself firmly in the female cloaca during mating. It is also very variable and so can help in identifying and classifying a snake. Most snakes have a pair of gonads – testes in males and ovaries in females – which lie asymmetrically in the elongated body, the right gonad always situated farther forward than the left. In the Brahminy and other blind snakes, the female has only a right ovary.

### BREEDING TIMES

Snakes normally breed each year, but, in cooler temperate regions where summers are short, they may only breed once every two or even three years to allow females to build up food reserves. Mating is thought to be triggered mainly by day length. The sex cells usually develop during the winter months, and, in temperate areas, many snakes mate in the spring soon after emerging from hibernation. Some, such as the Adder in northern Europe, mate in the fall before hibernation, and the embryos develop over the winter.

Embryos may not be formed immediately after mating, though, because certain conditions, such as a minimum temperature, are needed before snakes start to breed. The female can store sperm in the oviduct (the channel leading to the ovary) for several months until conditions are

*Adders* (Vipera berus) *mating (above right), the more contrastingly marked one being the male. Like some other snakes, the Adder performs elaborate courtship "dances" prior to mating.*

*Pine Snakes* (Pituophis melanoleucus) *mating with their bodies closely entwined (right). The male's hemipenis has backward-pointing spines, so during copulation the snakes cannot easily be separated.*

right. Captive female snakes have even been known to store sperm for several years, before eventually laying fertile eggs.

## COURTSHIP AND MATING

Snakes are usually solitary animals, have poor eyesight, are virtually deaf, and have no voice, so finding a mate is not always easy for them. As far as is known, snakes rely on a scent secreted from the anal glands to find each other, and a male follows the scent trail of any female in reproductive condition. Most snakes do not have the elaborate courtship displays seen in other groups of vertebrates, such as birds and mammals, however, some snakes, such as the Adder, perform mock-combat dances which appear to be closely linked with mating.

When male and female meet, the female usually remain passive. The male, tongue flickering, rubs his chin containing sensory tubercles along the hind part of the female's back. In boas and pythons, the male uses his clawlike vestigial hind limbs to stroke the sides of his mate. If the female is not receptive, she will move away. If she is, she responds with jerking movements, which may become more vigorous as the male moves forward until the two snakes' tails entwine and their two cloacas are adjacent to one another. Then the male inserts one of his hemipenis into the female, and the pair may remain joined for a short while or several hours. On separating, they usually go their individual ways. Males of some species insert waxy plugs after mating which remain in the female for a few days before falling out.

## EGG-LAYING AND BIRTH

The length of time the embryos develop inside the mother, or the gestation period, varies according to conditions, particularly temperature, and from species to species. The biggest difference is between those snakes that lay eggs and those that give birth to live young. Egg-laying snakes have a relatively short gestation period of about 30–85 days. Once laid, the eggs are incubated for a further period, usually about 40–90 days.

*Green Water Snakes* (Nerodia cyclopion) *(left) from the south-eastern U.S.A., where they are found in wooded swamps and other wetland habitats. This photograph shows males and females congregating prior to mating. They are among the most prolific snakes known, with the female giving birth to 100 or more young.*

The eggs are generally laid in shallow holes covered with a thin layer of soil. Some snakes lay their eggs under stones or in hollow logs or tree stumps. The main aim is to provide a site that is not too hot by day nor too cold at night, because the development of the eggs is directly related to their temperature. The European Grass Snake often lays its eggs among decaying vegetation, such as compost or manure heaps, where the heat generated by the decay provides a uniform temperature and excellent incubation. If suitable nesting sites are at a premium, snakes may nest together, and these communal nests may have hundreds of eggs in them.

Most snakes do not look after their eggs, but there are exceptions. The female King Cobra makes a two-chambered nest out of leaves and other vegetation. She deposits her eggs in the bottom chamber and occupies the upper chamber in order to defend the nest. All pythons coil themselves tightly around their eggs during incubation, and the Indian Python is able to raise its body temperature, and that of the clutch of eggs, several degrees higher than the surrounding temperature. Snake eggs are usually elongated and have thick, pliable shells, which are sticky when freshly laid and may adhere to one another. Each egg contains all the nutrients required for the full development of the young except water and oxygen, and these reach the developing embryo by diffusion through the shell. The hatchlings have a special tooth, known as an egg-tooth, with which they cut their way out of the shell. When the young snake has cut a hole big enough for its head to emerge, it often rests, sometimes for a whole day, before crawling out.

Other snakes retain their eggs within their bodies, until they are on the point of hatching, and then give birth to live young. These eggs have only a thin shell, since they are protected by the mother's body. A few snakes have even developed a simple placenta (a cord from mother to fetus), although probably only oxygen and water pass through it. Examples of live-bearing snakes are most sea snakes, some garter snakes, and the Adder. The gesta-

*A Taipan* (Oxyuranus scutellatus) *hatching (below). Most snakes lay eggs, usually with soft, leathery shells.*

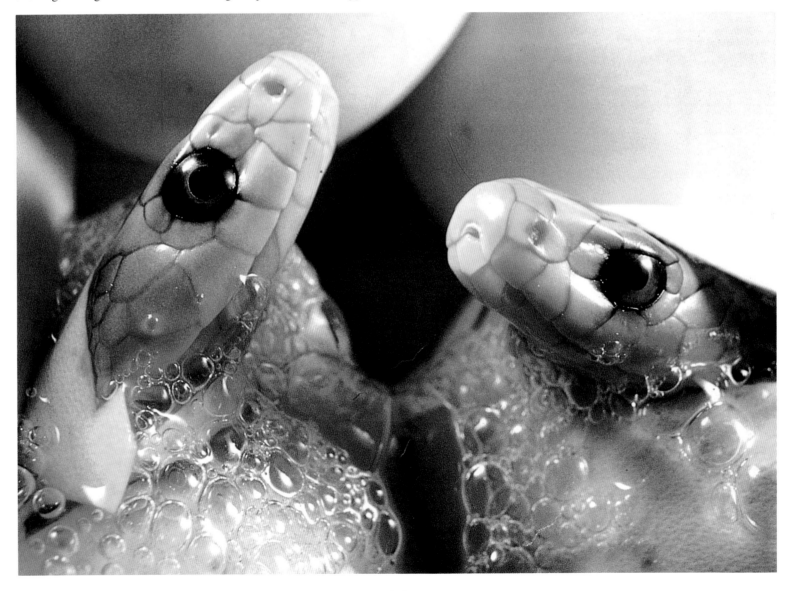

tion period of living-bearing snakes varies from about 90–150 days, occasionally more. The Boa Constrictor and the Adder, for example, have a gestation of 100–150 days, whereas in the Common Garter Snake (*Thamnophis sirtalis*), it is only 90–100 days.

A big advantage of live-bearing is that the female can control the temperature of the developing young, just as snakes control their own body temperature, by moving in and out of the sun. A major disadvantage is that as the eggs develop, they grow in size and become a distinct encumbrance to the mother, making her more vulnerable to predation. As a consequence, most live-bearing snakes tend, on average, to have smaller broods than egg-layers.

In some rattlesnakes, the young stay with their mother for some time and she will defend them. However, most snakes show little or no parental interest in their offspring, and many will even eat young of their own species. So most young snakes have to live independently immediately after they hatch or are born.

## GESTATION

There is considerable variation in the size of the brood within as well as between species. This is partly because the age and size of a female affects the number of eggs or young she is able to bear. The Indian Python, for example, lays 20–60 eggs, while the Plains Black-headed Snake *(Tantilla nigriceps)* only lays 1–3 eggs. Similarly, the Rubber Boa *(Charina bottae)* gives birth to only 2-8 young, whereas the Northern Water Snake *(Nerodia sipedon)* may give birth to 8-99 young.

## GROWTH AND LONGEVITY

Young snakes often have markings and coloration that are strikingly different from their parents, and they are surprisingly long at birth. The eggs of European Grass Snakes are only 1¼ inch (3 centimeters) long, yet the hatchlings that emerge are 6–7 inches (15–17 centimeters) long. Like all other snakes, they continue to grow throughout their lives, the rate of growth slowing with age. There is little reliable information on snake growth, but it is probably very variable, depending on such factors as temperature and food supply as well as age.

Snakes usually become sexually mature in their second, third, or fourth year, depending on the species and environmental conditions. Tropical snakes usually mature in under two years, whereas snakes in the more temperate northern regions do not mature until their fourth year.

It may be possible to tell a snake's age by examining growth rings in their bones. However, most information on the lifespan of snakes comes from observations of captive specimens.

## LONGEVITY RECORDS

The record for a Timber Rattlesnake *(Crotalus horridus)* is over 30 years and that for a California Mountain Kingsnake *(Lampropeltis zonata)* over 24 years. A Boa Constrictor is known to have lived for over 40 years, and an Indian Python for over 31 years. Obviously, these figures will not be typical of snakes in the wild, where life expectancy is usually much lower.

The Hognose Viper (Bothrops nasutus) *(left)*, a pit viper, giving birth to live young in the Costa Rican rain forest. The young hatch fully equipped with poison fangs, and, although they can only deliver a small dose of venom, it is just as toxic as that of the adults.

# FEEDING

All snakes are carnivorous and swallow their prey whole, which is often huge in comparison with the snake. It might be thought that snakes would have difficulty in catching prey since they have no limbs and generally have poor hearing and sight. However, they have evolved several specialized organs and techniques that more than compensate for these lacks.

The Rough Green Snake (right) lives on insects, such as this Lubber Grasshopper.

### TYPES OF PREY

Some snakes, especially the larger ones, show little discrimination and will eat almost any animal they can catch and swallow. The Western Terrestrial Garter Snake from North America, for example, takes tadpoles, frogs, worms, slugs, fish, mice, and small birds. Similarly, the Cottonmouth (*Agkistrodon piscivorus*), also from North America, will eat a wide range of animals, including frogs, fish, snakes, and birds.

Many snakes, though, concentrate on a small range of prey, and some are extremely specialized. The very small blind snakes (*Leptotyphlops*) eat just termites and ants, while the snail-eating snakes from South America (*Dipsas, Sibon,* and *Sibonomorphus*) feed on land snails. Some African snakes, such as *Dasypeltis scabra*, specialize in eating eggs, often very large in comparison with themselves. The Striped Crayfish Snake (*Regina alleni*) concentrates on crayfish, some sea snakes on fish, the King Cobra on snakes, while others eat only frogs, lizards, or rodents.

Many of the smaller snakes are insectivores, and the young of many larger snakes are only able to eat small prey at first, changing their diet as they grow. There is a limit to what even the largest snakes can eat. It has been reported that Reticulated pythons have eaten humans, but the only substantiated case occurred when a 14-year-old boy was found inside one. Nevertheless, such large snakes can consume pigs and small deer, and the Anaconda is reputed to attack and eat caimans up to 6 feet (1.8 meters) in size.

### CATCHING PREY

There are two main ways in which snakes catch prey – by actively hunting, or by sitting and waiting. The hunters are in the minority. They are often slender and fast-moving, such as the Coachwhip from North America, and rely on sight to detect their prey. For those that sit and wait, smell and heat detection (of warm-blooded prey) are important, and they tend to be heavy bodied and well camouflaged. Examples of these "lurkers" are the boas and pythons, vipers and pit vipers.

Many snakes, especially when young, have a brightly colored tail contrasting with the dull color of the

An Anaconda (Eunectes murinus) (opposite) constricting a caiman. Like all other constrictors, anacondas do not break the bones of their prey but suffocate it.

An African Egg-eating Snake (Dasypeltis scabra) (right and above), swallowing a bird's egg several times the size of its head. In order to do this, the snake's jaws dislocate, and spines in the neck slit the egg as it passes through the gullet. The egg is then crushed, and the shell is regurgitated.

37

rest of the body and use the tail as a lure. For example, the young Copperhead (*Agkistrodon contortrix*) from North America holds its bright-yellow tail vertically and twitches it, simulating a caterpillar. It feeds mainly on insectivorous animals, such as lizards and frogs, lured by the tail. As the snake grows, it focuses on different prey and loses this lure.

## SUBDUING PREY

Snakes eat most invertebrates, and smaller and weaker vertebrates, by simply swallowing them alive. Their backward-pointing teeth help prevent even slippery prey from escaping. Larger and more potentially dangerous prey are subdued by either constriction or venom.

It is well known that large boas such as the Anaconda and pythons such as the Reticulated Python kill their prey by squeezing it. What is less well known is that they do not crush their victim to death, but merely hold it tightly in their coils until it suffocates. Some snakes, instead, squeeze prey against an object before swallowing it.

Three families of snakes, the *Colubridae, Elapidae,* and *Viperidae,* have evolved separately the ability to produce venom and the apparatus to deliver it. Enlarged teeth have developed into fangs which are used to inject the poison into the prey. In their simplest form, the fangs have a groove down which the venom runs. In more advanced snakes, such as vipers and pit vipers, the fangs have evolved into a tube through which the venom is injected, like a hypodermic needle. Most poisonous snakes have the fangs at the front of the jaw and are said to be front-fanged. Examples are the Gaboon Viper, which has the longest fangs of any snake, and the Timber Rattlesnake.

In male vipers and viperids, the fangs are so long that they are folded backward on the jaw and swing down and forward when the snake opens its mouth to strike. Some snakes, such as the Boomslang and the Twig Snake, are back-fanged and have their fangs at the rear of the jaw. In all snakes, there are usually several fangs in reserve behind the main fang,

*A young Cottonmouth* (Agkistrodon piscivorus) *(above left) may use its brightly colored tailtip as a lure to attract fish.*

*An Eyelash Palm Pit Viper* (Bothrops schlegelii) *(middle and bottom left) photographed in Costa Rica. It is lying in wait for a Rufus-tailed Hummingbird, which on this occasion escaped.*

in various stages of development. The replacement of fangs takes place regularly, for example every three months in rattlesnakes, and the fang is often swallowed and excreted with the feces if it has not already been broken.

Saliva or digestive juices have been modified to form the venom. In the least poisonous snakes, the main purpose of the venom is still to aid digestion. In the more highly advanced – and more poisonous – species, its purpose is to kill prey as quickly as possible. Venom is a complex cocktail of toxins and so may damage the victim in a number of ways. For example, the neurotoxins in venom attack the victim's nervous system, especially the nerves of the respiratory system and the heart. Anticoagulants prevent clotting of the blood and cause profuse bleeding, while coagulants cause thrombosis or blood clotting.

Each species of snake has its own characteristic combination of these poisons, and this may even vary within a single species. In general, toxins affecting the blood dominate in viper venom, and neurotoxins in that of cobras and their allies. The strength of venom also varies from snake to snake, some being weakly toxic and able to kill a mouse, while others are highly toxic and able to kill an animal the size of a human. The most toxic poisons are those produced by the sea snakes. The most poisonous land-dwelling snakes are found in Australia.

Poisonous snakes can strike with amazing speed. The most advanced snakes of all, the vipers, stab while striking with fangs erected and facing forward. Predators use various tactics to evade the fangs, but they do get bitten from time to time, and some have developed a resistance to the venom of particular snakes. For example, rats can tol-

*A Fer-de-lance* (Bothrops godmani) *(left) photographed in the cloud forest of the Sierra Madre, Chiapas, Mexico, One of the most feared of all pit vipers, it has massive fangs, and its bite is fatal to humans.*

### VENOM AND SWALLOWING

The fangs of a boa (**1 and 2**) and a viper (**3 and 4**). In (**4**) the fangs are at rest, but in (**3**) they have swung down as the mouth opened, ready to strike. At rest, each fang is protected by a fold of mucous membrane, and behind them other fangs are growing. Diagram (**5**) shows the position of the poison gland, which is a highly modified saliva gland.

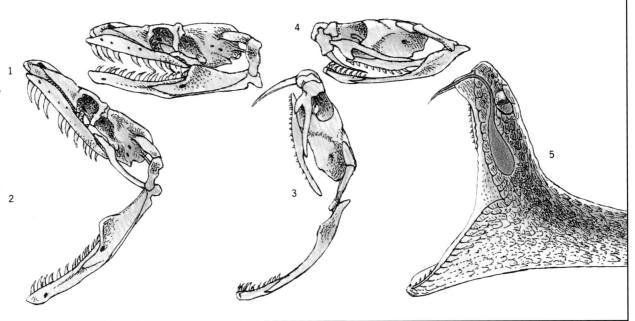

erate six times more Eastern Diamondback Rattlesnake (*Crotalus adamanteus*) venom than similarly sized guinea pigs, while the European hedgehog is 30–40 times more resistant to the venom of the Adder than a guinea pig. Some New World opossums and skunks have antibodies in their blood which neutralize the venom of pit vipers.

### SWALLOWING AND DIGESTION

Snakes lack the means to tear or dismember prey and so must swallow their victim whole. Relatively small prey is easily swallowed, and even larger prey poses few problems for most snakes, with the victim usually drawn in head first. The snake's mouth is extremely flexible, and the bones on both sides of the upper and lower jaws can move apart and even become dislocated from other bones of the head. These adaptations give the snake a very wide gape and allow it to swallow animals much larger than its head. The two sides of the jaws move independently when swallowing: one side holds the prey and the other side moves forward over it, guaranteeing that the prey does not escape. Swallowing may take a few seconds or several hours, depending on the size of the prey. In order to breathe while swallowing, the snake moves its windpipe forward past the victim along the floor of the mouth.

A snake may regurgitate recently swallowed food if, for instance, it is trying to escape from a predator. Otherwise, digestion may continue for several days or even weeks in the case of big prey. Snakes may go without food for up to a year after a large meal. They also fast during hibernation, when shedding their skin and, sometimes, when pregnant. Most prefer to drink regularly, but desert-living snakes can go without water for months or even years.

This Boomslang (Dispholidus typus) *(far left)* has captured a weaver bird at its nest. The free-hanging nests of weavers are safe from most predators, but a long, slender snake such as the Boomslang is able to extract the young birds, or even an incubating parent.

An African Python (Python sebae) *(left)*, which has killed and started to devour an impala in the Nairobi National Park, Kenya.

Its body distended after feeding, this Cascabel (Crotalus durissus) *will need several days to digest its prey (below). After a large meal, many snakes are able to fast for weeks or even months.*

# ENEMIES AND DEFENSE

The main enemy of snakes is undoubtedly humankind. Their wholesale destruction of the delicately balanced habitats of snakes and their killing of snakes for manifold reasons have made people the main threat to snakes throughout the world. Snakes have no defense against loss of habitat and little defense against humans determined to kill them. In the natural world, they are preyed on by numerous mammals, birds, and other snakes, but against these enemies they can often mount an effective defense.

## NATURAL ENEMIES

The legendary enemy of poisonous snakes is the mongoose, made famous by Rudyard Kipling in his tales of Rikki Tikki Tavi in *The Jungle Book*. Although the mongoose will indeed tackle venomous snakes, it prefers less risky food. In combat with a cobra, for example, the mongoose relies on its great agility and partial immunity to cobra venom, but the outcome of the fight is by no means a forgone conclusion. In misguided attempts to control large snake or rat populations, people introduced mongooses to other parts of the world, such as some Caribbean and other islands. There the mongooses found easier prey, with disastrous results for the local fauna, including the extinction of several birds species. Similarly, snakes usually form only a small part of the diet of the other mammals that prey on them, such as hedgehogs, cats, wild dogs, foxes, raccoons, pigs, and badgers.

Many birds occasionally eat snakes, including 33 species in Europe alone, such as herons, white storks, magpies, and jays. There are some birds, however, that eat snakes as a major part of their diet. Among the birds of prey that regularly hunt snakes are the Crested Serpent Eagle

*A Red-shouldered Hawk eating a snake (above right). Although birds of prey are not immune to venom, their feathers give them good protection from bites.*

*Secretary Birds at their nest, in Kenya (right). Secretary birds live in open savanna and are particularly adept at killing snakes, using their long, powerful feet to kick them to death.*

(*Spilornis cheela*), which ranges from India to the Philippines, and the Short-toed Eagle (*Circaetus gallicus*), which is found in Europe and Asia. The Congo Serpent Eagle (*Dryotriorchis spectabilis*) hunts snakes in the forests of west and central Africa, as does the White Hawk (*Leucopternis albicollis*) in the forests of South America. The Bateleur (*Terathopius ecaudatus*) soars above the savannas of Africa and will take, among other things, poisonous snakes, while even the widely distributed Golden Eagle (*Aquila chrysaetos*) may eat the occasional snake.

The Secretary Bird (*Sagittarius serpentarius*) is a very large, chiefly ground-living bird of prey that occurs in open grassy country in Africa. It includes snakes in its varied diet, often using its long, powerful legs to stamp them to death. The seriemas (*Cariama cristata* and *Chunga burmeisteri*) of South America are similar in many ways to the Secretary Bird and regularly eat snakes. The Roadrunner (*Geococcyx californicus*), a fast-moving ground cuckoo found in the southwest and Mexico, will take snakes, and the Laughing Kookaburra (*Dacelo novaeguineae*) of Australia, like almost all kingfishers, may eat small snakes.

Snake-eating snakes are quite common, and even cannibalism is not unknown. The large, poisonous King Cobra is a regular snake-eater and will eat smaller specimens of its own kind, as well as such poisonous species as the Banded Krait (*Bungarus fasciatus*). In Europe, both the Smooth Snake (*Coronella austriaca*) and the Southern Smooth Snake (*Coronella girondica*) have a taste for snakes. A number of North American species such as the Racer (*Coluber constrictor*) eat mostly small, nonpoisonous snakes, while the Indigo Snake and the Milk Snake (*Lampropeltis triangulum*) also eat venomous species. The Kingsnake includes in its diet the poisonous coral snakes, copperheads, and rattlesnakes. In South America, the harmless Massurana (*Clelia clelia*) eats the poisonous lance-head snakes (*Bothrops species*).

*Snakes often prey on each other (above). Some eat smaller specimens of their own kind, while others eat other species exclusively.*

## DEFENSE

Like most animals, the natural reaction of the majority of snakes when confronted by an enemy is to avoid being seen by remaining motionless, or to escape as quickly as possible and find cover. However, if snakes are disturbed while hungry or during the mating season, they will be more unpredictable and may become aggressive.

### CONCEALMENT

Snakes may use their color, pattern, shape, and posture to evade the eyes of predators. The snake's color and pattern may be similar to the background, such as in the green Long-nosed Tree Snake, which matches the foliage in its forest home in Southeast Asia. Alternatively, the color and pattern may be such that the animal's outline is lost. This disruptive color and pattern is exemplified by the Gaboon Viper, which is difficult to see in the tropical forests of Africa where it lives. Many snakes use a combination of these two types of camouflage.

### INTIMIDATION

In other snakes, though, color and pattern serve to advertise rather than conceal the animal's presence. The red, yellow, and black bands of the striking New World coral snakes (*Micrurus* and *Micruroides* species) make them stand out – and warn predators that these snakes are poisonous. Startling color signals are also given by the Ringneck Snake (*Diadophis punctatus*). When threatened, it coils its tail tightly and raises it up to show the brightly colored underside. This also diverts the would-be attacker away from the head. The Rubber Boa has a tail similar in outline to the head and, when threatened, it coils itself up tightly, with its head under the coils and its tail protruding on top. So if the predator does attack, it is likely to strike at the nonvital tail, leaving the snake free to make a surprise counterattack with its head.

A change in shape is another way to intimidate. The Boomslang inflates its neck, so making itself look bigger, while the Puff Adder blows up its whole body. The Cobra rears up the front part of its body and expands its hood. The Cottonmouth and the Bicuda (*Oxybelis aneneus*) threaten by opening their mouths to a wide gape. More aggressive behavior is shown by a number of snakes, including some North American species. The Northern Water Snake flattens its body and strikes repeatedly if cornered, while the Pine Snake (*Pituophis melanoleucus*) vibrates its tail, hisses loudly, and sometimes flattens its head before lunging at an intruder.

Many snakes use sound to intimidate, most commonly a loud hissing. Some, such as the African Egg-eating Snake (*Dasypeltis scabra*), can produce a grating sound by rubbing their scales together. Others, like the Fox Snake (*Elaphe vulpina*) from North America, vibrate their tails rapidly in surface litter. The best-known tail rattlers are, of course, the rattlesnakes, which vibrate the vertically held rattle at the ends of their tails to produce a buzzing sound that will scare off most would-be predators.

### FEIGNING

When concealment, warnings, and intimidation have failed, some snakes roll over and pretend to be dead. The Grass Snake from Europe will do so, but the strategy is best exemplified by the North American hognose snakes. For example, when the Eastern Hognose Snake (*Heterodon platyrhinos*) is disturbed, it inflates its body, hisses loudly, and strikes. If this fails, it

*A Cottonmouth* (Agkistrodon piscivorus) *opens its mouth in a threat display (right), exposing the vivid-pinkish interior of the mouth.*

will roll over limply with mouth open and tongue hanging out. Even turned the right way up, it will resume its "death" pose. It is difficult to see the point of this strategy, since many predators will eat freshly killed prey and carrion.

### OTHER STRATEGIES

Snakes commonly defecate if molested, the foul-smelling secretion from the anal glands presumably serving to deter an intruder. Among a host of other defenses is that used by the Black-necked Cobra (*Naja nigricollis*) and another African cobra, the Ringhals (*Hemachatus haemachatus*). These snakes forcibly eject venom, not from the tips of the fangs, but from openings at the front of the fangs. They can "spit" up to a distance of 11.5 feet (3.5 meters) and aim their venom with great accuracy at the eyes of a would-be attacker, rendering it temporarily – or even permanently – blind.

*The Monocellate Cobra* (Naja koovthia) *spreads its hood (above).*

*The Ringneck Snake* (Diadophis punctatus) *(left) can eject a foul-smelling liquid from its vent at an intruder. It may also display its brilliantly colored underside.*

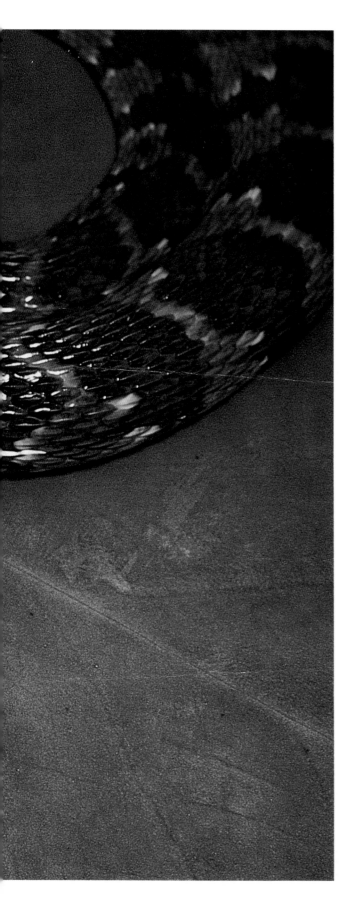

# SNAKE HABITATS

Snakes are found in virtually all natural habitats, and in a large number that have been modified by people or are entirely artificial. They are absent from Arctic tundra and most mountainous areas above the tree line. They are also absent from most urban areas, although some snakes do manage to survive in all but the most built-up environments, particularly in the tropics.

In general, snakes are more abundant and diverse in warmer habitats. They have adapted well to deserts, but it is in the tropical forests that they have flourished most. In common with other tropical-forest wildlife, each species of snake may occur in relatively low densities, but there is a great diversity of species. The differences which allow so many snakes to coexist in close proximity should present a fascinating area of research for biologists of the future – if the tropical forests and their wildlife survive.

*A young Southern Water Snake* (Nerodia fasciata), *photographed in Georgia (left). It occurs from South Carolina to Florida, where it is one of the more abundant aquatic snakes and may even be encountered in backyard pools.*

# DESERTS

All continents except Antarctica have substantial areas of desert, which together cover more than one-third of the world's land surface. In addition to hot deserts, such as the Kalahari and the Sahara, there are temperate and cold ones, such as the Gobi. Many deserts are such great distances from the seas that rain-bearing winds never reach them, but a few, such as in Chile and Peru, are adjacent to the sea. Contrary to popular belief, this habitat is not mainly sandy; bare rock and screelike debris form the greater part of most deserts.

Desert is one of the few habitats that is actually increasing in area. Soils in tropical forests are often thin and very specialized, and are not suitable for other uses after deforestation. Overcultivation can soon use up all the goodness in the soil, while overgrazing bares the soil to the elements. Irrigation frequently brings salts to the surface, making the soil unproductive after a few years. The end result of all these changes is often desertification, and some 46,000 square miles (120,000 square kilometers) of land are converted to desert each year.

Deserts receive small and erratic amounts of rainfall, usually less than 10 inches (250 millimeters) per year, and for most of the year they are dry. When rain does fall, it is often in violent thunderstorms, and dry watercourses and wadis become raging torrents for a few days. Immediately after rain, the desert bursts into a tapestry of color as wild flowers bloom, having remained dormant as seeds during the dry periods which can last for several decades.

Sandy deserts, such as parts of the Sahara, have little vegetation the rest of the time, but other deserts are well vegetated throughout the year. The Sonoran Desert of North America is a particularly lush example, even containing forests of small trees that are modified to carefully conserve the low rainfall and the heavy dew that forms at night. Plants lose water through their leaves, so in desert plants the leaves are reduced or not present at all; the stem takes over the production of food. Plants also conserve water by having waxy or thick leathery surfaces to reflect heat and retain moisture, and underground tubers or thick stems to store water. They may also be hairy in order to catch and retain moisture. Such modifications are typified by some of the most frequent forms of vegetation in deserts, the cacti. Perhaps the best

known is the giant Saguaro Cactus of the deserts of the southwest, and cacti occur in almost infinite shapes and sizes.

In summer, deserts are very hot during the day, reaching up to 134 degrees Fahrenheit (57 degrees Centigrade) in Death Valley, and cold at night. Perhaps surprisingly, many animals can cope with such extremes, and snakes have adapted particularly well to this harsh environment. The most obvious adaptations of desert snakes are that they are usually either active only at twilight or are nocturnal, and burrow under the ground where it is cooler during the heat of the day.

Certain features of snakes make them especially well suited to life in the desert. For instance, snakes do not pass liquid urine, instead secreting uric-acid crystals as a white paste with the feces, and they lack sweat glands in their skin. These features, together with the protective, impervious scales covering the body, allow snakes to conserve moisture. Snakes can go for a long time, even years, without drinking, obtaining the water they need by metabolizing fat in their food. As a result, desert species are found among many groups of snake, especially the vipers and pit vipers, the boas, colubrids, and cobras.

Many desert-dwelling snakes move by a special type of locomotion known as sidewinding (see p.26), which enables them to progress easily and rapidly over loose sand. They may also have rough scales, to give them a better grip on rocks. Desert snakes are often light colored to reflect the sun's rays and are frequently well camouflaged. Another adaptation seen in some is the development of protective "horns" above the eyes. These have evolved independently in several snake groups and can be seen in the Sidewinter Rattler from North America and the Horned Puff-adder and the Horned Viper of Africa. These snakes burrow

*The Namib Desert is among the most inhospitable areas of the world (right), but even there snakes manage to survive.*

in the sand and lie concealed from prey and predators with only their eyes and "horns" visible; the horns may act as lures for potential prey. Peringuey's Desert Adder, from Africa, has taken this one stage farther. It has eyes and nostrils on the top of its head so that, when it is concealed beneath shallow sands, it can still see and breathe.

*A Western Diamondback Rattlesnake* (Crotalus atrox) *in the Arizona Desert (above right).*

*The Badlands of South Dakota (left). In areas such as this with little or no fresh water, snakes rely on dew or the moisture in their prey.*

# MOUNTAINS

Mountains are present on all continents and, above 10,000 feet (3000 meters), even in the tropics, are generally inhospitable to snakes. Conditions in the montane habitat typically include low temperatures and high winds. Most serious for snakes in temperate regions are the low temperatures, both daily and seasonal. Snakes cannot survive where the ground remains frozen throughout the year, as it does at higher altitudes even in the tropics, and survival through the winter months is only possible where frost-free underground refuges can be found for hibernation.

At high altitudes and latitudes, the period during which snakes can be active is short. Very few snakes have managed to colonize both these harsh environments, but the Adder, one of the most widespread species in Europe, is found to latitude 68 degrees north in Scandinavia, crossing the Arctic Circle, and to an altitude of 10,000 feet (3000 meters) in the Alps. The vipers and pit vipers have managed to exploit the montane environment more than any other group, both in the Old and New World. For example, in Europe, the Asp Viper (*Vipera aspis*) and Orsini's Viper (*Vipera ursinii*) both occur up to about 10,000 feet (3000 meters) in the Alps. In Asia, the Himalayan Pit Viper has been found at greater altitudes than any other snake, living near the foot of a glacier in the Himalayas at a height of 16,000 feet (4900 meters). North America contains extensive mountain ranges, notably the Rockies and the Appalachians, which have a rich and varied snake fauna, including pit vipers such as the rattlesnakes.

---

**DISTRIBUTION OF SNAKES IN HONDURAS**

A study in Honduras showed a sharp fall in number of species with altitude. There were 65 species below 325 feet (100 meters), only 20 species between 4225-4550 feet (1300-1400 meters), 10 by 5525 feet (1700 meters), and at altitudes of over 7150 feet (2200 meters) only a single species, *Rhadinaea montecristi*, occurred. In other parts of Central America, the Mexican Dusky Rattlesnake *(crotalus triseriatus)* occurs up to 14,300 feet (4400 meters).

---

*The Dudhkosi Valley in the Sagarmatha National Park, Nepal (above), with the snow-covered Himalayas in the background.*

*Orsini's Viper* (Vipera ursinii) *(right) is a montane species found in the European Alps.*

*Mount Corvatsch, Engadin, Switzerland (far right). At high altitudes, only live-bearing snakes such as vipers can survive.*

# TROPICAL FOREST

Tropical forests are found in a broad belt around the world on both sides of the equator. They are essentially warm throughout the year and, because of the high rainfall, usually have a humid environment in which the vegetation is luxuriant and diverse; the Malay Peninsula alone has 2500 species of trees. The fauna is correspondingly rich and varied, and it is estimated that several million species of animals and plants live in the tropical evergreen forests. Many species still await discovery and scientific description, and certainly some of these will be snakes.

Prey is plentiful in tropical forests, and, since the air temperature is always relatively high, there is no need for snakes to hibernate, so they remain active throughout the year. In such favorable conditions, snakes have thrived, and of the 11 families of snakes, members of all but one, the wart snakes, are found in tropical forests in some part of the world. Unfortunately, this great variety of snakes is among the least known of any snake community in the world. Simply observing them is difficult, for there is usually plenty of ground cover, the vegetation can be almost impenetrable, and the snakes seldom emerge into the open. Even when they are exposed, their coloration may make them very difficult to see.

The forest trees are home to several arboreal snakes, which are often superbly camouflaged. Those living in the foliage may be green, such as the Long-nosed Tree Snake from the forests of Southeast Asia. Among the species which inhabit the forest floor, the Gaboon Viper from the tropical forests of Africa, has a superb disruptive, leaflike pattern, which renders it almost invisible on the dark forest floor and makes it very easy to tread on. This species is large, as are several of the other snakes found in tropical forests. The largest pit viper in the world, the Bushmaster (*Lachesis muta*), lives on the forest floor in South America. The two largest snakes in the world, the Anaconda from South America and the Reticulated Python from Southeast Asia and Indonesia, inhabit the "jungle" of the tropical forests. These huge snakes rely on the dense cover of the tropical forests to hide while they wait to surprise their prey. They take animals up to the size of peccaries, deer, and antelope and need several days or even weeks of inactivity, hiding in the forest, to digest their meal.

*Dense tropical forest in northern Thailand (right). Many species of arboreal snakes live there, but most have been little studied. In recent years, the construction of aerial walkways traversing the forest canopy has given scientists greater opportunity to study the wildlife.*

*The Green Tree Python (Chondropython viridis) (below) is a typical snake of the rain forest.*

### TROPICAL ADAPTATIONS
A number of snakes in very different parts of the world have adapted to their topical-forest homes in remarkably similar ways. For example, the arboreal Long-nosed Tree Snake parallels the Bicuda of the forests of South America, both being long, slender, and green in color. Equally similar in size, color and arboreal habit are the Emerald Tree Boa from South America and the Green Python living in New Guinea and north-eastern Australia.

*Rain forest (left) on the Arima River, Trinidad, in the Caribbean. In tropical forests, many snakes are confined to the upper levels, living their entire life in the canopy.*

*The Gaboon Viper (Bitis gaboni- ca) (right) from West Africa is a heavy bodied, superbly camouflaged species, closely resembling the leaf-litter of the forest floor where it lives.*

# TEMPERATE FOREST

In the cooler or more temperate latitudes, between 35 and 70 degrees north, lie the broadleaf and coniferous forests. The latter grow north of latitude 55 degrees and cover much of northern Eurasia and North America. The more southerly broadleaf forests contain a greater variety of trees with hardwoods predominant. Few survive in the northern hemisphere, though, for many of its broadleaf forests have been felled to make way for agriculture, towns, and industry, or to be replaced by conifers. In the southern hemisphere, temperate broadleaf forests only occur in southern Chile, New Zealand, Tasmania, and parts of Australia, while coniferous forests are virtually absent.

Fewer snakes inhabit the temperate than the tropical forests, fairly southerly Massachusetts, for example, having only 13 species. In the northern boreal forests, the dense canopy keeps the forest floor cool and gives snakes little chance of basking in the sun to warm themselves up. So very few snakes are found there, with, for example, only three species inhabiting southern Sweden and Norway. The colder winters in temperate latitudes force snakes to hibernate for periods lasting from a few months in the south up to nine months in the extreme north. Even during their active periods, there may be relatively little sun. So snakes in temperate regions tend to be smaller than in the tropics, needing less energy to warm up, and they may be darker in color or black, allowing them to absorb more of the sun's rays.

*Holm oaks (far right), such as these photographed in Hérault, France, were once widespread and typical of the Mediterranean. Much of Europe's forests have now been cleared for agriculture, which is in turn losing ground to urbanization.*

*Not all rain forests are found in the tropics. In the American northwest, there are spectacular temperate rain forests such as this (right) on the Olympic Peninsula of Washington.*

# GRASSLANDS

This habitat covers nearly a third of the world's land surface and includes vast stretches of modern grasslands, formed by the conversion of forests to grazing land and pasture. There are also "natural" old grasslands, such as the African savanna, South American pampas, North American prairie, and Eurasian steppes. These are characterized by low rainfall, cold winters, and warm summers. The most critical factor in the formation and maintenance of many of them are the fires which sweep across periodically, inhibiting tree growth. Once established, some of the old grasslands become home to huge herds of herbivorous mammals, such as those of the African savanna, and the bison that once roamed the North American prairies. Very few bison and very little prairie now exist, and the majority of the natural temperate grassland and steppes in other parts of the world have been destroyed or converted to agricultural use.

Many snakes live in the world's grasslands or adjacent habitats, such as grass scrub and open woodland. In North America, two species of *Lampropeltis* are found in prairie areas among other habitats, while the Western Hognose Snake (*Heterodon nasicus*) occurs in sandy and gravelly prairie, ranging from Canada through the central U.S.A. to Mexico. In South America, the Urutu (*Bothrops alternatus*) and the South American Rattlesnake (*Crotalus durissus terrificus*) are two of the species that inhabit grasslands. Snakes of the savanna, grass scrub, and woodland of Africa include the Puff Adder, which is one of Africa's best-known adders because it is widespread and often abundant. The Boomslang is a poisonous back-fanged snake of savanna areas of Africa, usually living in scrub and trees where it can be seen basking in the early morning and evening. The Taipan, one of the largest and most dangerous snakes in Australia, occurs in open savanna woodland.

An open grassland interspersed with sholatype forest in India (opposite). Cobras and many other snakes are commonly found in such habitats.

A baobab tree (left) in an open, lightly wooded savanna in Tanzania. The baobab is characteristic of the savannas of East Africa.

A Sonora Mountain King Snake (Lampropeltis pyrolemana) swallowing a lizard (below). The species is typical of more open prairies of the U.S.A., where it preys mainly on reptiles, including other snakes.

# RIVERS, LAKES, SWAMPS, AND SEAS

Freshwater and saltwater habitats cover by far the largest part of the world's surface. Few snakes inhabit both, although a few freshwater snakes may be found from time to time in salt water, while a few sea snakes may swim into estuaries and rivers. Freshwater snakes are present on all the continents (except Antarctica), and inhabit lakes, rivers, streams, swamps, marshes, canals, ditches, and ponds. Most snakes swim well, and even terrestrial snakes may take to water to avoid predators. Snakes swim with the same serpentine movement that they use on land, and many can stay submerged for considerable lengths of time without needing to surface for air.

Sea snakes are all members of the subfamilies *Hydrophinae* and *Laticaudinae*. They are restricted to the warmer waters of the Pacific and Indian oceans, and most occur in coastal waters. The majority hatch their eggs within the mother's body and give birth to live young at sea, and so never need to come on land. All sea snakes are poisonous but they are seldom aggressive, and the few fatal attacks recorded have been mainly against fishermen who have brought sea snakes up in their nets. Another feature they all share is a lateral flattening of the tail, which enables them to push against a greater volume of water and so propel themselves better. Occasionally, large gatherings of sea snakes are seen, but the reasons for these aggregations, as with many other aspects of their behavior, are not understood.

*A marsh in southern France (left) where snakes such as the Viperine Snake (*Natrix maura*) are found.*

*The endangered San Francisco Garter Snake (*Thamnophis sirtalis tetrataenia*) (below), which is threatened by the loss of wetlands in the San Francisco Bay area.*

The Mississippi Green Water
Snake (Nerodia cyclopion)
(above) is rarely found far from
water and is often abundant.

Salt marsh (top right) in the
Camargue on the Rhine delta in
southern France.

Swamps such as this (right) in
Georgia are rich in amphibians
and numerous snakes that prey
on them.

# SNAKES OF THE WORLD

Snakes occur in most parts of the world, including the seas. The following geographical survey is intended to reflect the diversity of snakes and so does not give even coverage to all regions. Within the geographical regions, there is often a very wide range of habitats, and only the more important and characteristic of these are mentioned, together with a representative selection of their snakes. While a few snakes have been well studied, little is known about the majority of the world's snakes other than their approximate distribution and what can be gleaned from a few pickled specimens in museums.

*A King Snake* (Lampropeltis getulus) *(left) photographed in the high plains of Texas. This species occurs over the southern part of the U.S.A. and Mexico in a wide variety of habitats, but particularly prairies and deserts.*

# NORTH AMERICA

Of the approximately 2700 species of snake in the world, 127 are found in North America. The vast majority, over 100 species, are colubrids (typical snakes), and they are mainly nonpoisonous. Other nonpoisonous snakes found there are two species of boa and two blind snakes. The 20 poisonous snakes include 17 pit vipers, two coral snakes, and one sea snake. Since 1950, there have been no more than 10 to 25 deaths annually from snake bites in the U.S.A., despite far more people having been bitten than in the past.

Snakes have managed to colonize almost every habitat in North America and occur from sea level to altitudes of over 10,000 feet (3000 meters). As might be expected, relatively few are found in northern latitudes, with only 23 species of snake occurring as far north as Canada, and none reaching Alaska.

### THE ARID SOUTHWEST

The border between Mexico and the southern U.S.A. does not follow any natural boundary for most of its length, and so the extreme south of the country contains several species which are more commonly associated with Mexico. They include the Glossy Snake (*Arizona elegans*), the Western Blind Snake (*Leptotyphlops humilis*), the Mexican Hook-nosed Snake (*Ficimia streckeri*) and the Twin-spotted Rattlesnake (*Crotalus pricei*). The large expanses of desert in the southwest have a particularly rich reptile fauna, including the only North American species of poisonous lizard, the Gila Monster (*Heloderma suspectum*). The Texas Blind Snake (*Leptotyphlops dulcis*) inhabits rocky or sandy deserts among other habitats and is found from sea level to 5000 feet (1500 meters). This highly specialized snake eats only termites and ants. It is seldom seen on the surface, for it is a nocturnal, burrowing animal, which only grows to 10½ inches (27 centimeters) long. A larger, stouter snake of the desert areas of Arizona and California is the Rosy Boa (*Lichanura trivirgata*), growing up to 42 inches (1.06 meters) long. This nocturnal snake may climb trees, but it lives mainly on the ground and feeds on small mammals and birds. It gives birth to live young and has been known to live up to 18 years in captivity, although little is known about the lifespan of this and most other snakes in the wild.

The rattlesnakes (pit vipers) are probably the best known of all the North American snakes. They are popularly associated with deserts, but, in fact, occur in a wide range of habitats. Rattlesnakes give birth to live young and generally prey on small mammals, such as kangaroo rats, birds, lizards, and small snakes. They locate their warm-blooded prey by means of heat-sensitive pits situated between the eyes and the nostrils (see p.29).

Among desert-dwelling rattlesnakes, one of the most strikingly patterned is the highly poisonous Mojave Rattlesnake, which has beautiful markings of brown diamonds down its back, outlined in white. The most familiar is the Sidewinder Rattlesnake, famous for its sidewinding method of locomotion (see p.26), by which it can move rapidly over loose desert sands. It has a hornlike projection over each eye and can grow up to 32 inches (82 centimeters) long. The largest western rattlesnake is the Western Diamondback Rattlesnake, a heavy bodied

species with a large head. It is found in desert and rocky areas, and its bite can be fatal to humans.

Several rattlesnakes are also found in rocky habitats in the mountains of the southwest. Among these are the Rock Rattlesnake, a medium-sized snake which occurs at altitudes of up to 9600 feet (2900 meters). The Speckled Rattlesnake (*Crotalus mitchelli*) is found up to altitudes of 8000 feet (2450 meters). It is very variable in color, usually harmonizing well with its surroundings. Its back may be any shade from cream to brown, and its markings usually consist of diamond-shaped or hexagonal blotches or crossbands. Among the least-known snakes of the southwest is the Black-tailed Rattlesnake (*Crotalus molossus*), which may grow to 49¼ inches (1.25 meters) and range up to altitudes of 9000 feet (2750 meters). The Twin-spotted Rattlesnake has a very limited distribution, only occurring in mountains at altitudes of 6300-10,000 feet (1900-3000 meters).

The Trans-Pecos Rat Snake (*Elaphe subocularis*) is a large species which constricts its prey of small mammals, birds, and lizards. It is found in the Big Bend and Trans-Pecos areas of Texas and New Mexico, and, like nearly all the desert species of the southwestern U.S.A., is also found south into Mexico. The large Glossy Snake gets its name from its smooth, lustrous scales. Ranging from California eastward to Texas, it is a snake of open areas, including deserts and grasslands, and feeds almost entirely on lizards. Little is known about another snake of the region, the small Banded Sand Snake (*Chilomeniscus cinctus*), except that it appears well modified for desert life. With its streamlined body, it is able to "swim" through fine sand, and it has valves on its nostrils which prevent dust from getting into them.

*A desert landscape in Monument Valley, Utah (above left).*

*The Rosy Boa* (Lichanura trivirgata) *(left) is found in arid habitats from southern California and southern Arizona to Mexico.*

*A Black-tailed Rattlesnake* (Crotalus molossus) *with pits clearly visible (above).*

*The Western Diamondback Rattlesnake* (Crotalus atrox) *(right) is one of the more aggressive rattlers, and its bite can be fatal to humans.*

One of the ways of avoiding the heat of the day is to retreat underground, and many desert-dwelling snakes have a head or snout specially adapted for burrowing. The Western Shovelnose Snake (*Chionactis occipitalis*) is a small desert species with valved nostrils and smooth scales. Its shovel-shaped head helps in burrowing, and it feeds by night on scorpions, insects, and centipedes. The closely related Sonoran Shovelnose Snake (*Chionactis palarostris*) is also a small, nocturnal burrower. Its bright colors, with red and black crossbands on a yellow ground, mimic those of the highly poisonous coral snakes. The Desert Hooknosed Snake (*Gyalopion quadrangularis*) burrows using its upturned snout. It is a secretive, nocturnal animal, and little else is known of its habits or life cycle. The Big Bend Patchnose Snake (*Salvadora deserticola*) and the closely related Western Patchnose Snake (*Salvadora hexalepis*) can tolerate higher temperatures than most other snakes. Both have an enlarged scale curved back over the snout. Similarly, the Spotted Leafnose Snake (*Phyllorhynchus decurtatus*) and the Saddle Leafnose Snake (*Phyllorhynchus browni*) have triangular patchlike scales on their snouts which enable them to push their way through sandy soil.

Of the two species of coral snake in North America, one is found in desert habitats of the southwest. The small, highly poisonous Arizona Coral Snake (*Micruroides euryxanthus*) preys on small snakes, including blind snakes. It is brightly colored, with black, red, and yellow or white alternating bands, and a black head. This "warning" coloration, typical of all the highly poisonous coral snakes, is mimicked by several nonpoisonous colubrids in North America, including the Sonora Mountain Kingsnake (*Lampropeltis pyromelana*). Found up to heights of 9100 feet (2800 meters), it has alternating bands of red, black and yellow or white along its body.

*A Mojave Rattlesnake* (Crotalus scutelatus) *photographed in southeastern Arizona (above left). This species has a particularly toxic venom, which causes severe respiratory problems. It is found in deserts with cacti, mesquite, Joshua trees, and similar vegetation.*

*A Sonora Whip Snake* (Masticophis bilineatus) *in southeastern Arizona (left). This very long, slender snake is adapted for climbing in bushes and trees, where it preys on lizards and nesting birds.*

# THE ROCKIES AND THE WEST

The Rockies span a particularly diverse area of North America and contain large areas of wilderness, much of it protected in some way. Geologically, they are a relatively young series of mountains with frequent earthquakes. Many of the volcanoes are still active, and the most recent major volcanic eruption was that of Mount St. Helens (1980). The protected Yellowstone region is in an area of constant volcanic activity, the most famous signs of which are its hot volcanic geysers, especially Old Faithful. Habitats in the Rockies range from permanent snow to arid desert, and include prairies, coniferous and broadleaf forests, and even temperate rain forests. Offering such a wide variety of habitats, the area has a rich fauna, including many snakes.

The large Western Rattlesnake may be found in the Rockies at higher altitudes than any other snake in North America, ranging from sea level to 11,000 feet (3350 meters). It is an aggressive species, with a wide distribution in the Rockies of the western U.S.A. and Canada, occurring as far north as southern Alberta, southwestern Saskatchewan, and southern

*A Rubber Boa (Charina bottae) coiled up in its defense posture (right). It has a wide range in the western U.S.A. and north into British Columbia.*

*The beautifully marked Striped Whipsnake (Masticophis taeniatus) (left). Like other whipsnakes, it is extremely fast.*

British Columbia. In the northern areas of its range, large numbers of western rattlesnakes may overwinter together in a communal den. As with other communally hibernating species, this practice may be due to a shortage of good hibernating sites and may also help to maintain an even temperature.

The Striped Whipsnake (*Masticophis taeniatus*) is a large, fast-moving species found in a wide variety of habitats up to 9400 feet (2850 meters). It feeds on small mammals and lizards, and small snakes, including poisonous ones. One of the more frequently observed species throughout the Rockies is the Western Terrestrial Garter Snake. This day-active snake can often be found basking in the morning sun from sea level to 10,500 feet (3200 meters) over much of the western U.S.A. and Canada, as far north as southwestern Manitoba and southern British Columbia. It is found in a variety of habitats, including open grassland and forest, but usually near water. The closely related Northwestern Garter Snake (*Thamnophis ordinoides*) is also small and diurnal and, like all garter and ribbon snakes, it gives birth to live young. It is confined to the U.S.A. and west of Canada.

The Rubber Boa is sometimes known as the "two-headed snake," because its tail is shaped like its head. This may tempt an attacking predator to strike at the tail by mistake, leaving the more important head end alone. It is a good climber, burrower, and swimmer, and feeds on small mammals and lizards. The small Sharp-tailed Snake (*Contia tenuis*) grows up to 19 inches (48 centimeters) and, as its name suggests, its tail has a sharp spine at the end. It is a secretive snake of moist environments in western areas of the U.S.A. and Canada.

*A Western Terrestrial Garter Snake* (Thamnophis elegans) *photographed in Yellowstone National Park, Wyoming (above left).*

*Spotted phase of a Prairie King Snake* (Lampropeltis calligaster). *A typical prairie snake, it occurs over most of the eastern U.S.A. in a wide range of habitats and is generally unobtrusive, hiding by day and most often seen after rainstorms (above right).*

### THE PRAIRIES OF CENTRAL NORTH AMERICA

Only small pockets now remain of the vast areas of prairie grasslands that once spread over most of central North America and were inhabited by millions of buffalo, antelope, elk, and bighorn, and by the native Americans who hunted them. It is thought that these areas were maintained as open prairie for thousands of years largely by wildfires and fires started deliberately by the native Americans. When European settlers arrived, the land management changed, and within less than a century the prairies were reduced to isolated remnants.

Prairie habitats can also be found in the Rockies, Florida, and elsewhere. There are two main types of prairie – tall grass and short grass – and considerably more of the latter remains than the former. The scarcer tall-grass prairie, which is lush and full of flowers in spring, survives in pockets at unlikely sites such as railroad embankments and cemeteries.

Several species of snake inhabit the prairie grasslands of central North America, including the Prairie Kingsnake. This slender, secretive, medium-sized snake is also found in a wide range of other habitats. It spends most of the day hidden underground, in burrows, in loose soil, or under rocks, and its prey includes other snakes. The closely related Milk Snake is also secretive, eats snakes among other prey, and is found in a wide range of habitats, including prairies, from sea level to 8000 feet (2450 meters). It is larger than the Prairie Kingsnake, up to 78¼ inches (1.99 meters), and is very variable in appearance, being gray, brown, or red with white or yellow and black rings on the body.

The Western Hognose is a small snake found in prairie grasslands from sea level to 8000 feet (2450 meters). Like all hognose snakes, it may feign death when attacked, although not as readily as some of its relatives. When playing possum, the snake rolls over on its back and lolls with mouth agape. Unfortunately, if it is turned the right way up, it often gives itself away by trying to turn upside down again!

### THE APPALACHIANS

The Appalachians are a series of separate mountain ranges that run from Canada through the eastern U.S.A. south to Georgia, and are among the oldest mountains in the world. Dividing the east coast from the central plains, they formed a natural barrier to the westward expansion of the English colonies until the independence of the U.S.A. Then the mixed hardwoods forests that covered the mountains were heavily logged, and now they have been largely replaced by farmlands or secondary forests.

Among the snakes found in the Appalachians is the large Timber

A closeup of the head of a Western Hognose Snake (Heterodon Nasicus) *showing the shovel nose used in burrowing (opposite, top left). During the heat of the day, this snake burrows in loose soil, where its acute sense of smell enables it to locate food such as toads and reptile eggs buried underground.*

The Ribbon Snake (Thamnophis proximus) *has a distinctive striped pattern, which provides camouflage in its grassland habitat (opposite, top right).*

The Timber Rattlesnake (Crotalus horridus) *(opposite, bottom right) is one of the most widespread of all North American rattlers, occurring in many habitats.*

The head of a Pine Snake (Pituophis melanoleucos) *(above). It has a wide range in North America, from Alberta and Saskatchewan in Canada through much of the U.S.A. to Mexico.*

*Long-needled pine and palmetto in southern Florida (top right). This habitat, characteristic of much of Florida, is favored by Eastern Diamondback Rattlesnakes* (Crotalus adamanteus).

*A closeup of an Eastern Diamondback Rattlesnake (above), showing the characteristic patterning that gives rise to its name.*

Rattlesnake, which is widely distributed in the central and eastern U.S.A. It is becoming increasingly rare in many areas, particularly close to human settlements. Like the Western Rattlesnake, the Timber Rattlesnake may overwinter in large numbers in northern areas, sometimes mixed with North American rat snakes (*Elaphe*) and copperheads. The Copperhead's North American range is similar to that of the Timber Rattlesnake and includes the Appalachians. Both snakes are pit vipers, and the Copperhead's bite is painful, although only very rarely fatal to humans. It is a stout-bodied snake, coppery or orange in color, with bold reddish-brown crossbands. A nonpoisonous snake commonly found in the Appalachians, and in other parts of the U.S.A. and Canada, is the secretive Ringneck Snake. Superficially very similar to the Grass Snake of Europe, this small, slender snake has a pale-yellowish neckband. It also has a brightly colored underside, which it may flash when disturbed.

## FLORIDA

Florida offers a range of habitats, including pine flatwoods, tropical hammocks, and swamps, and much of it is subtropical. As a result, a wide variety of reptiles inhabit the state. Unfortunately, many alien animals have now been introduced and are thriving.

The pine flatwoods are found in low-lying, often swampy, areas with numerous shallow lakes and ponds, and they form open woodland with good ground cover for snakes. The plants that grow there, such as the Florida slashpine, are well adapted to cope with the wildfires that regularly sweep through the underbrush. Among the snakes associated with

pine flatwoods is the Pine Woods Snake (*Rhadinaea flavilata*), a small, secretive creature which eats frogs and lizards.

The Eastern Diamondback Rattlesnake is a large and particularly attractive species, with diamond-shaped markings down the middle of its back. It is also the most dangerous snake in North America, for its venom destroys blood and tissue, and can cause human fatalities. This snake is now declining rapidly in Florida due to land developments and persecution. During rattlesnake "roundups," people gassed gopher-tortoise burrows, which are among the rattlesnake's main retreats. The now illegal practice of gassing also decimated the gopher tortoises and affected the many other animals that take refuge in their burrows, including small mammals, burrowing owls, gopher frogs, toads, and invertebrates.

Another snake that inhabits gopher-tortoise burrows and so has seriously declined in Florida is the nonpoisonous Eastern Indigo Snake (*Drymarchon corais couperi*). It is the largest snake in North America, growing to 103½ inches (2.63 meters). The Eastern Indigo Snake is found in a variety of habitats, including the tropical hammocks of Florida. These raised pieces of ground, usually amid wet areas, contain mainly evergreen hardwoods such as mahogany and strangler fig. The trees form dense canopies over a floor covered with ferns and rotting vegetation, and epiphytes and lianas may also be present, giving the hammocks a "tropical" appearance. Much of the habitat has been destroyed in recent years. The Rim Rock Crowned Snake (*Tantilla oolitica*) is a little-known species only known from tropical hammocks on (oolilitic) limestone in Florida and the upper Florida Keys. Less than 9¾ inches (24 centimeters) long, this nocturnal species is the rarest snake in Florida and possibly the

rarest in the whole of North America. Only a few specimens have ever been found, and little is known about its habits.

In addition to the famous Everglade swamp, Florida has a very wide variety of other freshwater habitats, including swamps, ponds, lakes, streams, rivers, and canals. Aquatic snakes are found in all of these, and among those characteristic of the region is the Striped Crayfish Snake (*Regina alleni*). This small, shy snake is restricted to southern Georgia and Florida, where it occurs especially in water choked with water hyacinth, an introduced water plant. The Striped Crayfish Snake captures crayfish in its coils and restrains them while they are being swallowed. The Florida Green Water Snake (*Nerodia floridana*) is a large, aggressive species which frequents lakes, ponds, swamps, and sloughs. It is quick to bite, defecate, and spray musk at an attacker. The Swamp Snake (*Seminatrix pygaea*) is more timid and rarely bites when handled. It is found in swamps, cypress ponds, canals, and drainage ditches, again especially in areas overgrown by water hyacinth. One of the most common poisonous snakes in the region is the Florida Cottonmouth (*Agkistrodon piscivorus conanti*), which may be found around almost any freshwater habitat in Florida and on many of the keys. It rarely bites people, but when it does, the venom can prove fatal.

## CANADA AND THE NORTHERN U.S.A.

Over 20 different species of snake have been recorded in Canada, but most are restricted to the southern areas, often only just ranging over the U.S. border. The most northerly is the Common Garter Snake, which reaches a latitude of 67 degrees north in the Yukon, Canada. In northern latitudes, snakes can only be active for a short time during the year and have an extended hibernation period. Some overwinter together in larger groups, and those of the Common Garter Snake may number 8000 to 10,000. As with the Western Rattlesnake, they probably do this to help maintain constant body temperatures and overcome the lack of suitable dens.

In western Canada, the Rubber Boa occurs in southern British Columbia, as does the Racer (*Coluba constrictor*), as well as being present in the extreme south of Ontario. The Western Rattlesnake is found in southern Alberta, Saskatchewan, and British Columbia. The Common Garter Snake occurs in southern areas from the east to west coasts, making it the most widespread snake in Canada. Several other garter and ribbon snakes are found in southern Canada, including the Western Terrestrial Garter Snake (*Thamnophis elegans*), Butler's Garter Snake (*Thamnophis butleri*), the Northwestern Garter Snake, the Plains Garter Snake (*Thamnophis radix*), and the Eastern Ribbon Snake (*Thamnophis sauritus*). This group of live-bearing snakes has been the most successful of any in North America at extending its range into Canada. In eastern Canada, the Massasauga (*Sistrurus catenatus*) is found in southern Ontario, the Milk Snake in southern Ontario and Quebec, and the Brown Snake (*Storeria dekayi*) also in southern Quebec. The Redbelly Snake (*Storeria occipitomaculata*) extends from Nova Scotia in the east to southeastern Saskatchewan in the west.

The states of the northeastern U.S.A. have only a few snakes, but some of these occur nowhere else. The Short-headed Garter Snake (*Thamnophis brachystoma*), for example, is restricted to Pennsylvania and New York State. This small, live-bearing species inhabits old fields and meadows, and feeds on earthworms and small amphibians. Among the snakes restricted to northern areas of the U.S.A. is Kirtland's Snake (*Clonophis kirtlandii*). A small, slender snake, it is usually found near water, but is rarely seen actually in it, despite being a good swimmer. Another snake found in central northern areas of the U.S.A. is the harmless Fox Snake. Its range extends from the Great Lakes region west to South Dakota, Nebraska, and northern Missouri, and it occurs in marshland and dunes around the lakes, prairies, farmland, and wooded valleys. This large snake is often mistaken for the poisonous Copperhead and killed.

*A Short-tailed Snake* (Stilosoma extenuatum) *(opposite, far left), on a tropical-hardwood hammock in Florida. This species is confined to the Florida Peninsula.*

*The large Indigo Snake* (Drymarchon corais) *(opposite, right) is threatened by the destruction of gopher-tortoise burrows, in which it frequently hides.*

*The Southern Water Snake* (Nerodia fasciata) *(below) is common in a wide variety of aquatic habitats, including brackish waters.*

# MEXICO, AND CENTRAL AND SOUTH AMERICA

Perhaps the best known of this region's wide range of habitats are the vast tropical rain forests of Amazonia. It is there that the legendary giant boids are found, such as the Anaconda and the Boa Constrictor. The rain forests, more correctly described as tropical moist forests, extend over much of Amazonia and as far north as Central America. Arid areas are also extensive in the region, particularly in Mexico and along the Andes in Peru and Chile. The other main habitat in South America is the grassland, or pampas, of southern Brazil and Argentina. The number of snake species decreases farther south, and only a single species, the pit viper, *Bothrops ammodytoides*, occurs at the extreme south.

Although over 500 species of snake are known from Central and South America, the vast majority have never been studied in any detail in their natural habitat. Little is known about most of them except for their main identification characters and their rough distribution. In addition to the known species, there are certainly many more as yet undescribed. Large tracts of South America have never been explored by zoologists, and many exciting discoveries are likely to be made there.

## MEXICO AND CENTRAL AMERICA

The main habitats of this area are the deserts in the arid north of Mexico and the tropical rain forests. There are also extensive wetlands, and numerous active volcanoes and mountains, with most of Mexico at an altitude of over 3300 feet (1000 meters).

Much of Central America is extremely densely populated and has been cleared for agriculture. Although the agricultural areas are not as rich in wildlife as the natural habitats they replaced, some snakes do manage to survive in them, including the Terciopello (*Bothrops asper*). This large pit viper is very common and is the cause of most snakebites in the region, and so has many different local names. In addition to being known as Terciopello in Costa Rica, Nicaragua, Panama, and Venezuela, it may be called the Yellow-jaw Tommygoff in Belize, the Fer-de-Lance in Trinidad, and the Barba Amarilla in Honduras, Mexico, and Belize. Like all pit vipers, the Terciopello has heat-sensitive pits to locate warm-blooded prey.

There are around 60 species of poisonous snake occurring in Mexico, more than in any other country in the New World. Among these are

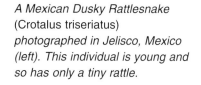

A Mexican Dusky Rattlesnake (Crotalus triseriatus) photographed in Jelisco, Mexico (left). This individual is young and so has only a tiny rattle.

Godman's Montane Pit Viper (Bothrops godmani) is well-camouflaged, its pattern mimicking that of dead leaves (right and above).

about 26 species of rattlesnake, many more than elsewhere in North America, or in Central and South America. The Mexican Lance-headed Rattlesnake (*Crotalus polystictus*) is especially common in Mexico in rocky areas with gopher burrows, in which it often hides. Gophers are small, desert-dwelling rodents which form a regular part of the diet of this and other rattlesnakes. The Mexican Dusky Rattlesnake (*Crotalus triseriatus*), a snake of upland areas, is found up to 14,300 feet (4400 meters), the highest altitude yet recorded for a snake in the New World. The Cross-banded Mountain Rattlesnake (*Crotalus transversus*) is small, growing to 18 inches (46 centimeters). It has a restricted distribution, only being known from a small area of the Sierra Ajusco, south of Mexico City, and fewer than 20 specimens have been found, all at altitudes of 9,360 feet (2900 meters) and above.

The arid, desert-dominated peninsula of Baja California has a particularly rich reptile fauna, which includes several rattlesnakes. One of these, the Rattleless Rattlesnake (*Crotalus catalinensis*), occurs only on the tiny island of Santa Catalina off western Baja California. It sheds its tail segments along with the rest of the skin and so, unlike other rat-

tlesnakes, it does not develop a rattle. Rattlesnakes are most diverse in northern Mexico, and in the extreme south only one species of rattlesnake occurs, the Cascabel or Neotropical Rattlesnake (see p.85).

There are 14 species of poisonous Porthidium pit vipers, largely confined to Mexico and Central America, but also ranging into northern South America. The smaller species account for 10–15 percent of snakebites in Costa Rica, but their venom is rarely fatal to humans. One of these, the Jumping Pit Viper (*Porthidium nummifer*), has many local names, including Jumping Tommygoff in Belize. It is found throughout much of Central America, inhabiting rain and cloud forests. Its name comes from greatly exaggerated claims that it can hurl itself large distances when striking at prey.

All but one of the seven species of palm pit vipers (*Bothriechis*) are confined to Central America. The exception is the Eyelash Palm Pit Viper (*Bothriechis schlegelii*), which has a range extending into northern South America. Like its relatives, it is a tree-living snake and is easily identified by its large "false eyelashes." These are spiny horns made up of two or three enlarged scales, projecting upward above the eyes.

The function of these distinctive features is unknown. The Eyelash Palm Pit Viper has exceptionally long fangs and, because it lives in low palms and bushes at human-head height, it usually strikes people on the face, arms, or hands. However, its bites are rarely fatal.

In contrast, the venom delivered by the large fangs of the Cantil (*Agkistrodon bilineatus*), an aggressive pit viper, has caused human deaths, sometimes in a matter of hours. This heavy-bodied snake can grow to 4½ feet (1.38 meters) and ranges widely in Central America. It usually prefers to live near water, like its close relative in North America, the Cottonmouth, but it is sometimes found far from permanent streams and ponds.

Among the most diverse group of snakes in Central America are the 54 species of poisonous coral snake. These are found in a variety of habitats, ranging from desert to cloud forests, and occur from the southwestern U.S.A., through Central America and over most of South America. Coral snakes are New World members of the elapid family, related to the cobras and mambas of the Old World. As their name suggests, they are often brightly colored, usually bearing alternating bands of black, red, and yellow or white, or some other combination. Their bright coloration is thought to act as a warning to would-be predators that these snakes are poisonous. Few of them grow to more than 5 feet (1.5 meters), and all have relatively small hollow front fangs which are rigidly fixed in the jaw and so are always erect (unlike those of the vipers, which are hinged and lie flat when the mouth is closed). Their venom is very potent, mainly attacking the nervous system, and can be fatal to humans. The coral snakes occurring in Central America include Allen's Coral Snake (*Micrurus alleni*) and Brown's Coral Snake (*Micrurus browni*). Some species have a very restricted range, such as the Tuxtlan Coral Snake (*Micrurus limbatus*), which is only found in a small area of southern Mexico.

Central America is also home to many nonpoisonous snakes, including the milk snakes. These harmless snakes probably gain some protection from predators by having banded patterns very similar to those of coral snakes (see p.44). Milk snakes and their close relatives, the snake-eating kingsnakes, are widespread in Central America. Both are very popular as pets, and, although the North American species are more usually kept, the Central American species are also sought, and several are now bred commercially.

Some species are very useful to humans because they prey on rats and other pests. Among these is the Central American Whipsnake (*Masticophis mentovarius*), which hunts mostly rats, mice, lizards, and small snakes. This harmless, fast-moving snake grows up to 7 feet (2.13 meters). The Indigo, or Blacktail Snake, is another large snake, growing to 8½ feet (2.6 meters). Also found in North America, it too is an important rat catcher and has a liking for snakes, including poisonous ones.

## AMAZONIA

The vast basin of the Amazon stretches from the Andes in the west to the east coast of South America, and includes the whole of northern Brazil as well as large parts of Peru, Colombia, Bolivia, and Ecuador. The tropical forests of the Amazon basin are probably closest to most people's idea of a "jungle," for they teem with plant and animal life of all kinds, and their remoter parts have never been explored. Sadly, these forests are currently being destroyed at an alarming rate, with hundreds of thousands of acres burnt to make way for agriculture each year.

The best known of the many snakes found in the Amazon Basin are the Anaconda and the Boa Constrictor. Also occurring in the Orinoco Basin, the Anaconda is most famous for its huge size. The largest-known specimens are an impressive 30 feet (9 meters) long, but exaggerated accounts of their size abound. The claim by the famous explorer Colonel Fawcett that he killed a 62-foot (19-meter) specimen has never been believed, and there are even absurd reports of this snake growing to 140 feet (43 meters). A dead specimen is often skinned, and the ease with which snakeskin stretches has almost certainly contributed to such stories.

The Anaconda is the most aquatic of all the boas and is often abundant in areas of the Amazon that are inundated periodically. It is never found far from water and prefers slow-moving or still waters, particularly favouring swamps. On land it is usually sluggish. In the water it can swim rapidly, but is often seen floating motionless, lying in wait for its prey. The Anaconda's diet consists of birds, fish, and small mammals, including peccaries, deer, and large rodents such as capybara. More rarely it will take turtles, and there is even a report of a large Anaconda killing a 6-foot (1.83-meter) caiman.

Among the folklore surrounding the Anaconda are tales of man-eating specimens, but there is very little evidence to support these. Stories also tell of the Anaconda breaking every bone in its prey's body. In reality, few or no bones are broken when the prey is constricted, for the Anaconda kills prey by suffocation rather than crushing it. The snake's mouth is adapted so that the upper and lower jaws come apart, allowing it to swallow prey wider than itself. After a meal of a large animal, such as a deer, the Anaconda may not eat again for several days or weeks, until the meal is completely digested.

The Boa Constrictor is not restricted to the tropical forests and so has a much wider distribution than the Anaconda. It ranges as far north as Mexico, where it is found in more arid habitats, and as far south as Argentina. It also occurs on Trinidad and a few other islands of the Lesser Antilles, and on the coastal cays of Mexico and Belize. Unlike the Anaconda, the Boa Constrictor has no special preference for water and often climbs trees. It grows up to 14½ feet (4.5 meters), but is perfectly harmless to people. This large, well-camouflaged snake has much in common with other boas. It moves so slowly that it has to wait for its prey to come to it, rather than chasing it, and then kills the prey by constriction. It gives birth to live young, and there are usually 20–60 young per brood, each about 20 inches (50 centimeters) long. The Boa Constrictor has been known to live for over 40 years in captivity.

Along with most other tropical snakes, there is very little information available on current population levels of the Boa Constrictor and Anaconda. The Boa Constrictor is thought to be seriously depleted in Argentina and El Salvador, while remaining abundant in other parts of its range. In some areas it is encouraged and protected because it helps to control rats and mice. Probably the main threat it faces is being hunted for its skin. For example, as many as 100,000 snakes a year may have

*The Cascabel or Neotropical Rattlesnake (Crotalus durissus) (opposite left) is a large rattlesnake widespread in savannah and other habitats of Central and South America, as far south as Brazil and Argentina.*

*An Ornate Palm Viper (Bothrops aurifer) (opposite right), a brilliantly colored arboreal pit viper from Mexico and Guatemala.*

*An Amazon Tree Boa (Corallus) (left) hides in the fork of a tree, striking at birds or arboreal mammals as they pass by.*

# SOUTH AMERICAN SNAKES

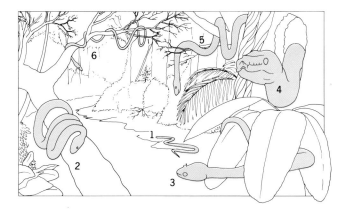

Much of South America was covered with tropical forest, and, although it is disappearing at an alarming rate, it still covers hundreds of thousands of square miles. Vast tracts of these forests have never been explored by biologists and almost certainly contain many as yet undiscovered species of animals, including snakes. The Anaconda (1), a constrictor, is among the largest snakes in the world. It kills animals up to the size of deer, peccaries, and caimans, and often spends its time immersed in water waiting for prey to come and drink. Many tropical snakes are brilliantly patterned (2) and look conspicuous in zoos, but their bright colors often provide excellent camouflage in the depths of the forest, where shafts of sunlight contrast with dark shadows. Many arboreal snakes (6) are extremely long

and slender, which provides camouflage among slender twigs and enables them to climb from branch to branch with agility. The pit vipers use their heat-sensitive pits to detect prey and are generally rather slow-moving snakes, relying on camouflage to surprise their prey. Some South American pit vipers (3) are arboreal, as are the boas (2, 4, and 5). Many species of arboreal snake spend the day hanging in branches above rivers and pools and will simply drop into the waters if they are disturbed by a predator.

1 Anaconda 20-25ft (6-7.5cm)
2 Rainbow Boa 6ft (1.8m)
3 Schlegel's Pit Viper 2ft (60cm)
4 Emerald Tree Boa 11ft (3.4m)
5 Cook's Tree Boa 6ft (1.8m)
6 Bicuda 5ft (1.5m)

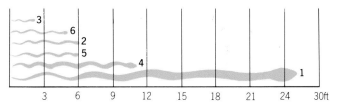

been taken between 1980 and 1983. The problem is aggravated by the fact that large skins are in greatest demand, and so it is the mature breeding snakes that are being removed from the populations. Young boas are also in demand for the pet trade, with 18,418 exported from South America in 1985. Similarly, mature Anacondas have been hunted for their skin, while small specimens are collected for the pet trade. Its relative, the Yellow Anaconda (*Eunectes notaeus*) has also suffered heavily, with 37,000 specimens traded in 1984, most originating from Paraguay, Bolivia, and Argentina. All three of these snakes are listed in Appendix 11 of the Convention on International Trade in Endangered Species of Fauna and Flora (C.I.T.E.S.), which means that export permits are required for any commercial trade.

Another Amazonian boa, the Emerald Tree Boa, is an arboreal snake which is only occasionally seen on the ground. It has a bright-green upper side with irregular white markings and a yellow belly and feeds on birds and tree-living mammals. When at rest or lying in wait for prey, it characteristically drapes its coils over a horizontal branch.

The area is also inhabited by many poisonous snakes, including the Common Lancehead (*Bothrops atrox*), which is found throughout most of Amazonia. There are 31 species of lancehead in South America, all of which are poisonous, and many of which contribute to human deaths in the area. Of the 2000 deaths each year attributed to snakebites in South America, the Common Lancehead is believed to be responsible for a third, mainly because it has potent venom and is especially abundant near human habitations. It is a fairly heavy bodied pit viper which can grow to 6½ feet (2 meters). Although it is primarily a ground-living snake, the Common Lancehead will readily climb trees.

Brazil's Lancehead (*Bothrops brazili*) has a very similar overall range to the Common Lancehead, but is restricted to primary forests where it lives among the leaf litter. Fonseca's Lancehead (*Bothrops fonsecai*) is confined to a relatively small area in southeastern Brazil, occurring in well-drained areas in the Atlantic forest zone. Since this is one of the most threatened habitats in South America, and Fonseca's Lancehead is only known from a few observations, it may be at risk. Other lanceheads with restricted ranges include the Golden Lancehead (*Bothrops insularis*), which is only known from the small island of Queimada Grande off southeastern Brazil, where it is apparently abundant, and the White-tailed Lancehead (*Bothrops leucurus*), only known from a tiny area in Bahia, Brazil. Some of these snakes and several other related pit vipers with very restricted ranges may turn out to be merely variants of more widespread species. Alternatively, the vast forests of Brazil are being destroyed so fast that there may be no time to find out more about these snakes nor to study the others that doubtless await discovery.

Virtually all the pit vipers in the New World bear live young. The only known exception is the Bushmaster, which lays eggs. This heavily built snake is the longest pit viper in the world, growing to 11½ feet (3.6 meters). It lives on the forest floor in tropical rain forests, usually in areas that receive more than 166 inches (400 centimeters) of rain a year, although it can occur in much drier habitats. It is found throughout most of the Amazon Basin and in other areas of northern South America and Central America. A separate population inhabits the coastal forests of eastern Brazil. The Bushmaster is not usually aggressive, but it is wide-

*A Green Tree Python* (Chondropython viridis) *(right) on the island of New Guinea, hanging in a characteristic pose with its coils looped around a branch.*

*A Yellow Anaconda* (Eunectes notaeus) *photographed in the Ibera Marshes, Argentina (opposite left). Anacondas spend much of their life submerged in water, and larger specimens feed on deer and other animals as they come to drink.*

*The Boa Constrictor* (Boa constrictor) *(opposite right) is one of the most widespread of all South Americans snakes, living in a great variety of habitats. Like the anacondas, larger specimens spend much of their time in water.*

*The Emerald Tree Boa* (Corallus caninus) *(right), from the rain forests of Brazil, occasionally hunts on the ground, but is more usually found in trees, where its brilliant green coloring gives it excellent camouflage.*

*An Amazon Rat Snake* (Elaphe) *(left). The extremely rich and diverse snake fauna of the Amazonian rain forests has not been studied in detail, and little is known about even common species such as this one.*

ly feared, probably partly because of its size. Also, like other heavy bodied pit vipers, it lies in wait on the forest floor, relying on its superb camouflage to enable it to surprise prey, and so it is relatively easy to step on.

The Two-striped Forest Pit Viper (*Bothriopsis bilineata*) is one of eight closely related species of forest pit viper in South America. Most of these are arboreal snakes which climb using their long prehensile tail. The Two-striped Forest Pit Viper has a wide range in northern South America, including Amazonia, and is most abundant in lowland rain forest, especially near water. It is a relatively small, slender, green snake, usually less than $3^{1/3}$ feet (1 meter) long. It is most frequently encountered in shrubs, trees, and vines, often at about head height, and so is the cause of many severe bites to humans.

There are many poisonous coral snakes found in South America, including Langsdorff's Coral Snake (*Micrurus langsdorffi*), which can grow to 2½ feet (76 centimeters) long. It occurs in the Upper Amazon Basin, where it inhabits lower montane wet forest and lowland rain forest. Langsdorff's Coral Snake may be banded in two or three colors, and this variation in markings makes the snake very difficult to identify. Often it has bands of red (which may become black) alternating with yellow, brown, or black, and each ring is separated from the others by a narrow row of white spots that becomes a narrow band on the belly. The closely related Amazonian Coral Snake (*Micrurus spixii*) has a wide range in northern South America, including Amazonia. It lives mainly on the floor of tropical rain forests and is one of the largest coral snakes, growing up to 5¼ feet (1.6 meters). Despite being perhaps the best known of all South American coral snakes, very little is known of its habits. The Aquatic Coral Snake (*Micrurus surinamensis*) is also fairly large. It is an adept swimmer and inhabits the tropical rain forests of Amazonian South America, usually along streams or rivers. Like many

coral snakes, it has alternating bands of red, black, and yellow.

Among the more specialized snakes found mainly in the tropical forests are the mollusk-eating snakes. The three groups, *Dipsas*, *Sibon*, and *Sibonomorphus*, are confined to South America and feed only on slugs and snails. They are arboreal, mostly nocturnal snakes and are very rarely seen during the day as they hide among the epiphytes and other vegetation of the rain forest.

Perhaps the least known snakes in South America are the 20 or so species of thread snakes belonging to the genera *Liotyphlops*, *Anomalepis*, *Helminthophis*, and *Typhophis*. These tiny snakes live almost exclusively underground in the forest litter, and very little is known of their habits or even their precise distribution.

### THE ANDES AND THE WEST

The western edge of South America is home to a number of unique snakes. This is because the great Andean mountain chain, which runs along the entire length of western South America, forms a formidable barrier for snakes and other wildlife to cross. Western Peru and Chile contain areas, often close to the sea, where rain rarely falls and many of the rivers dry up. Several species of coral snake are found in these deserts, including the Desert Coral Snake (*Micrurus tschudii*). It inhabits the semiarid Pacific coast of South America, from southern Ecuador down through Peru. This diurnal snake is tricolored with red, black, and yellow alternating rings and may climb trees. Steindachner's Coral Snake (*Micrurus steindachneri*) is found along the eastern slopes of the Andes in Ecuador. Also tricolored, it inhabits lower montane wet forest and cloud forests. Many coral snakes are known only from very restricted areas, such as another tricolored one, Peter's Coral Snake (*Micrurus petersi*). Only two specimens of this snake have ever been found, both in the Rio Upano Valley region of Ecuador in cloud forest and lower montane wet forest.

Two little-known forest pit vipers occur in the Andes of Ecuador. The Ecuadorian Forest Pit Viper (*Bothriopsis albocarinata*) inhabits cloud forest in the high Andes, up to an altitude of 10,000 feet (3000 meters). This snake has only been found in two places, and its habits are virtually unknown. The closely related Andean Forest Pit Viper (*Bothriopsis alticola*) is only known from a single small specimen found near Loja in Ecuador at an altitude of 9100 feet (2800 meters). These two snakes are very similar, and it is quite possible that they are isolated examples of the same species.

Several venomous lanceheads inhabit the Andes and Peru. The Desert Lancehead (*Bothrops pictus*) is found in arid and semiarid coastal deserts in the foothills of the Andes in Peru. Its venom is dangerous to people and has caused human deaths. Although presently classified as a separate species, Roedinger's Lancehead (*Bothrops roedingeri*) is only known from one coastal foothill desert in Peru and may be just an isolated population of the Desert Lancehead. A third lancehead, Barnett's Lancehead (*Bothrops barnetti*), is a very little-known species that has been recorded at low altitudes in the coastal deserts of northern Peru.

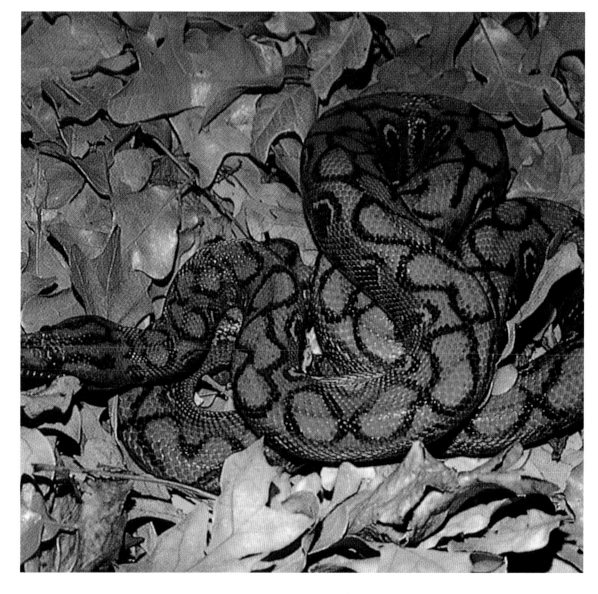

*A Bushmaster (Lachesis muta) (opposite left) lying camouflaged on the floor of a Costa Rican rain forest.*

*An Eyelash Palm Pit Viper (Bothrops schlegelii) (opposite right) photographed in Pichincha, Ecuador. It occurs from Belize south to Ecuador and Venezuela, mostly in tropical moist forest.*

*The Rainbow Boa (Epicrates cenchria) (left) is extremely variable, and several well-marked subspecies occur within its range, which extends from Nicaragua south to Brazil and Argentina. The genus Epicrates is widely distributed in Central and South America and also in the Antilles, where distinct species occur on several of the islands.*

## THE SOUTH

Southern South America, east of the Andes, is characterized by semiarid areas and grasslands or pampas. The grasslands spread from the tropics of the Mato Grosso down to the desolate, windswept area around Tierra del Fuego. One of the most dangerous snakes found in the region is the Cascabel, or Neotropical Rattlesnake (*Crotalus durissus*). This species occurs widely in semiarid areas of Central and South America, as far south as Argentina. It is unlikely to be misidentified because it is the only species of rattlesnake throughout most of its range, only overlapping with other rattlesnakes in Mexico. In addition, it can grow to 6 feet (1.8 meters) and has distinctive markings, with a series of large diamond-shaped blotches down its back and stripes on the neck. The most dangerous of all the rattlesnakes, its venom attacks both the blood and nervous system, and has caused many human fatalities. For example, in Brazil, 72 percent of people bitten by the Cascabel used to die. Between 1966 and 1973, since the introduction of antivenin, this figure has been reduced to 6 percent.

Two species of poisonous lancehead are found in the grassland areas of southern South America. The Urutu occurs in Brazil, Paraguay, Uruguay, and Argentina. It likes swampy areas, but also lives in a wide variety of other habitats including, in Argentina, open fields and rocky areas. This large, heavy bodied snake can grow to 5½ feet (1.69 meters) long and is a major cause of snakebites throughout its range. Although its venom can produce severe symptoms in people, the bites seldom result in death. The Patagonian Lancehead (*Bothrops ammodytoides*) is found farther south than any other snake, its range extending at least as far as southern Santa Cruz in Patagonia. It is one of six pit vipers that occur in Argentina, the others being restricted mainly to the north of the country.

The nonpoisonous colubrid snakes of the genus *Philodryas* are widespread, occurring mainly in open habitats, where they often live in burrows of the viscacha, a rodent. Their prey includes other snakes, as well as rodents, tree frogs, lizards, and ground-dwelling birds.

# EUROPE

The snake fauna of Europe is comparatively small, consisting of a mere 29 species. Nine are poisonous vipers, eighteen are nonpoisonous colubrids, and there is a single boa and a single blind snake. There are no elapids (cobras and their allies) nor pit vipers in Europe at present.

The landscape of Europe has been modified by people for several millennia, and very little totally natural habitat survives. In the colder areas, the British Isles, and much of northern Europe, only three species of snake are found – the Adder, the European Grass Snake, and the Smooth Snake. Unlike many other islands of comparable size and climate, Ireland is totally devoid of snakes. In warmer areas, though, particularly on the three peninsulas reaching into the Mediterranean and the numerous Mediterranean islands, snakes are often abundant.

## MEDITERRANEAN ISLANDS

There are more snakes in the Mediterranean than anywhere else in Europe because its warm climate suits snakes particularly well. Their watertight skins prevent dehydration, and the dry heat enables them to warm up their bodies to the required temperature levels quickly. Not surprisingly, sun-loving North African snakes thrive here. Snakes such as the Blunt-nosed or Levantine Viper (*Vipera lebetina*) and the Algerian Whip Snake or Racer (*Coluber algirus*), which originate in North Africa, have almost certainly been introduced by humans to the islands.

In Europe, the Blunt-nosed Viper is rather small, seldom growing to more than 2½ feet (80 centimeters). It is confined to the western Cyclades in the Aegean, occurring on Milos, Kimolos, Polygos, Siphnos, and possibly Kithnos and Antimilos. It is also found in southwestern Asia and northern Africa, where it may grow to a larger size (see p.98). In Europe, it is found mainly along damp or dry rocky stream beds, among adjacent scrub vegetation, and on rocky outcrops. It is of particular interest because its method of reproduction can vary. While in Europe it lays eggs, in some other parts of its range it gives birth to live young.

The venom of this snake is less toxic than that of a cobra, but large quantities may be injected and it acts very quickly. The venom attacks the blood and, unless the victim is treated quickly, may be fatal. The venom is also widely used in medicine. It has been estimated that there are about 8000-9000 adult vipers in the Cyclades (excluding Siphnos), and 90 percent of these are on Milos. Until 1977, there was a bounty system in which local people were given a nominal sum for each viper killed. This system no longer operates, but some vipers are still killed and many more (probably 1000-1500) are collected each year for sale abroad. Disturbance and destruction of its habitat due to opencast mining on Milos also poses a serious threat to the continued existence of this snake in Europe.

The Algerian Racer occurs in northwestern Africa and in Europe, where it is confined to Malta. It is uncommon in Malta and is usually

The Smooth Snake (Coronella austriaca) *(left) is declining in many parts of its range. Active during the day, it favors sunny, dry habitats.*

A Cat Snake (Telescopus fallax) *(right, above) on the island of Santorini (Thira), Greece. About 5000 years ago, a volcanic explosion destroyed all the life on the island, so this species must be a relatively recent colonist.*

A pair of European grass snakes (Natrix natrix) *(right) photographed in England. One of the most widespread and abundant snakes in Europe, it has declined in many parts of its range, possibly due to the clearing of river banks and the disappearance of farmyard manure heaps.*

found in dry, stony places, in rockpiles, and among ruins. This slender colubrid can grow to 3¼ feet (1 meter), but it is usually smaller. It is a yellowish snake with narrow black crossbands along its back from the head to the tail. Active during the day, it raises the front of its body off the ground to look for the lizards and small rodents on which it feeds. It approaches the prey carefully and slowly, but if the victim takes flight, the snake will chase it, moving at great speed over short distances.

In Europe, the Cat Snake (*Telescopus fallax*) is restricted to Malta, Crete, some of the Greek islands, and Adriatic Yugoslavia and the southern Balkans. It also occurs in the Caucasus and southwestern Asia. This poisonous, back-fanged colubrid has vertical, catlike pupils, but probably gets the name Cat Snake from the way it stalks its prey. Its smooth body scales readily distinguish it from the vipers, which also have verti-

cal pupils but keeled body scales. The Cat Snake is usually found in rocky places and feeds entirely on lizards. Its venom can kill small prey in a few minutes, but is not dangerous to humans.

Distinctive subspecies of the European Grass Snake occur on Corsica and Sardinia. This suggests that they colonized these islands a considerable time ago, almost certainly without human help. However, the snakes on some islands are very similar to their mainland relatives and are distributed rather arbitrarily, suggesting that they are comparatively recent arrivals. For instance, the Ladder Snake (*Elaphe scalaris*, see p.95) occurs on Minorca, but not in the rest of the Balearics.

## THE BALKANS

Until the 1960s, much of southeastern Europe was untouched by modern agriculture. The Danube Delta, the rivers and lakes of Yugoslavia and Greece, and the mountains of Romania, Bulgaria, and Greece had large remnants of wilderness with healthy populations of the wildlife that was once abundant and widespread in Europe. Although rapid industrialization has taken its toll and the rapid spread of tourism has destroyed many superb coastal habitats, the area still remains one of the best in Europe for seeing snakes.

The blind snakes are a primitive group, comprising about 200 species worldwide. In Europe there is only one species, the Worm Snake (*Typhlops vermicularis*), and this is confined to the southern Balkans and a few Greek islands. It also ranges eastward through southwestern Asia, the Caucasus, and northeastern Egypt. It is a wormlike, burrowing snake which grows to a maximum of 13½ inches (35 centimeters) long and is usually smaller. Its scales are smooth and glossy, and the inconspicuous head has tiny eyes which are only capable of distinguishing darkness and light. The tail is thicker than the head, and so enemies are inclined to confuse the two and attack the tail. Blind snakes like dry, open habitats, where they feed mostly on ants and their larvae. These snakes are seldom seen on the surface, except at twilight or in wet weather.

The Javelin Sand Boa (*Eryx jaculus*) has a similar range in Europe to the Worm Snake, being confined to the southern Balkans and a few Greek islands. It is also found in southwestern Asia and northern Africa.

The only boa found in Europe, it bears little resemblance to its giant New World cousins such as the Anaconda and Boa Constrictor. It only grows to 31 inches (80 centimeters) and is a burrower, seldom seen above ground. It is well suited for life underground, having a wedge-shaped head for burrowing, a blunt tail, and smooth, shiny scales. Like all boas, it gives birth to live young and kills its prey by constriction. It feeds mainly on small rodents, lizards, and nesting birds, and sometimes takes slugs.

Dahl's Whip Snake (*Coluber najadum*) and the Balkan Whips Snake (*Coluber gemonensis*) are two of the colubrids found in the Balkans. Both these fast-moving snakes are active during the day and grow to a maximum length of 3⅓ feet (1 meter). Dahl's Whip Snake, the more slender of the two, is found in Greece and some of its islands, southern Bulgaria and Yugoslavia, particularly along the eastern shores of the Adriatic. It also occurs in the Caucasus and southwestern Asia. It likes dry, stony habitats, usually with some grass or other vegetation, and feeds on small lizards and grasshoppers. The Balkan Whip Snake occurs on the eastern Adriatic coast, Greece, and Gioura in the Cyclades. If threatened, it will hiss loudly and strike at its enemy, and it bites fiercely when handled.

The Nose-horned Viper (*Vipera ammodytes*) gets its name from the single hornlike protuberance on the end of its snout. This highly poisonous snake is one of the most dangerous of the European vipers. It is widespread over a large area of southeastern Europe, including the Balkans, and southwestern Asia. This viper occurs in a wide variety of habitats, but prefers dry and sunny situations with stony ground and some vegetation. It often hibernates in large numbers, usually in rock fissures or underground cavities.

## ITALY

The habitats in the Italian Peninsula range from the Alpine meadows of the north to the arid, desertlike areas of Calabria in the south. Centuries of human activity have destroyed most of the natural habitats, but some of the new ones created, particularly olive groves, are favored by several species of snake. Although a few species of reptile and amphibian are restricted to the Italian Peninsula, all the snakes found there also occur elsewhere. Some are shared with the Balkans and eastern Europe, while others range into Iberia and northern Europe.

Orsini's Viper occurs in Italy and in Austria, Hungary, Romania, Yugoslavia, Albania, and Bulgaria, as well as Asia Minor and western Asia. The populations in Europe are often small, isolated, and diminishing in number. Many of these are so distinct from each other that they are said to be subspecies, and some may merit being separate species. In Italy, Orsini's Viper is restricted to the central Apennines, in the vicinity of Marche, Umbria, and Abruzzo, where it is at risk from collecting and habitat loss. It is probable that within historical times it was very much more widespread and abundant, but it has been ruthlessly persecuted because of its close resemblance to more poisonous species of viper. In fact, it is the least dangerous and smallest of the European vipers, being placid by nature and only growing up to 2 feet (60 centimeters) long. It is

*A Javelin Sand Boa (Eryx jaculus) (below) on the island of Amorgos, in the Aegean Sea. Europe's only boa, it is short-bodied and burrows in soft sand.*

*Closeup (right) of the head of a Nose-horned Viper (Vipera ammodytes) showing the spectacular outgrowth of scales on the nose tip, the function of which is not fully understood.*

found at higher altitudes than most other European snakes, up to 10,000 feet (3000 meters) in the Alps.

The handsome Leopard Snake (*Elaphe situla*) is relatively rare and appears to be decreasing over most of its range, which includes the Balkans, some Aegean islands, Malta, the southern Crimea, and Asia Minor and the Caucasus. In Italy it is localized, confined to the south and Sicily, and is decreasing in range. It is an attractively patterned snake, particularly when young, often having a row of black-edged red spots on its back and smaller spots on its sides, but sometimes bearing black-edged, reddish stripes. Its markings and coloration are remarkably similar to those of the Corn Snake (*Elaphe guttata*) from North America. Like all species of *Elaphe*, it kills its prey by suffocating the victim in its coils.

The related Four-lined Snake is widespread in southern Italy, and also occurs in southeastern Europe and southwestern Asia. As with many rat snakes (*Elaphe*), the juveniles may be markedly different from the adults. The young are usually boldly spotted at birth, and this pattern may continue into adulthood, or it may fade to form the four dark stripes along the back that have given rise to this snake's name. It is one of the largest European snakes, growing to a length of 8 feet (2.5 meters). A muscular, slow-moving, diurnal snake, it has keeled scales and is adept at both climbing and swimming. It feeds on small mammals, nesting birds, and eggs, and is often found along wood edges and hedges. Throughout much of its European range, the Four-lined Snake is localized, and populations are decreasing. This is mainly due to habitat destruction, overcollecting, and being killed as vermin. Another factor which may be affecting populations is road traffic, for snakes often bask on roads in the early morning or evening, avoiding the heat of the day, and some motorists deliberately drive at them.

Other snakes that occur widely in the Italian Peninsula include the Smooth Snake, the Southern Smooth Snake, the Aesculapian Snake, the Dice Snake (*Natrix tessellata*), and the Western Whip Snake (*Coluber viridiflavus*).

# EUROPEAN SNAKES

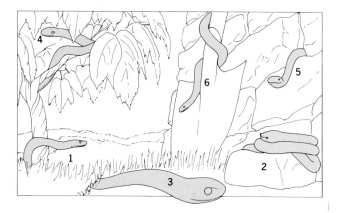

Most European habitats have been heavily modified by people, and the species of wildlife, including snakes, that still flourish are those that are adaptable and can survive in humanmade habitats, such as farmlands and hedgerows. Several of the many species of reptile that were relatively abundant and widespread in Europe until the present century have declined dramatically over the past 50 years. Since individual snakes are often relatively longlived, it can take several years to detect population declines. Orsini's Viper (1) occurs in meadows, but changing agriculture, as well as persecution, have made this relatively harmless viper one of Europe's most endangered reptiles. The more poisonous Nose-horned Viper (2) occurs widely in many drier habitats. Europe's most widespread snake, the Grass Snake (3), generally prefers wetter habitats. It lays its eggs in heaps of rotting vegetation, such as those deposited along river banks or compost heaps, and dunghills in farmyards. The Southern Smooth Snake (5), which preys mostly on lizards, has adapted to a number of humanmade environments, including vineyards and backyards. Some species have attractive markings, such as the Horseshoe Snake (4), often found around drystone walls, and the Leopard Snake (6). Snakes are often very territorial, and a snake seen basking on a particular heap of stones can usually be found there at the same time on most days, and may even return to the same spot year after year.

1 Orsini's Viper 20in (50cm)
2 Nose-horned Viper
  2½ ft (76cm)
3 Grass Snake 3-4ft (1-1.2m)
4 Horseshoe Snake 4ft (1.2m)
5 Southern Smooth Snake
  2ft (60cm)
6 Leopard Snake 3ft (1m)

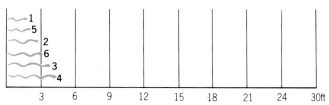

### IBERIAN PENINSULA

Iberia includes Spain, Portugal, and the tiny principality of Andorra, and is one of the best areas in Europe for seeing a wide variety of snakes. Isolated from the rest of Europe by the Pyrenees, it has several species of snake that are more or less confined to the region, and others that may also be found elsewhere in Europe and in North Africa. Many of the Iberian Peninsula's habitats have been heavily degraded, and it contains extensive areas of desert where some of the world's hottest temperatures have been recorded. In contrast, there are also many mountainous areas that have lush meadows and are snow-covered for several months of the year.

The Horseshoe Whip Snake (*Coluber hippocrepis*) is a handsome snake usually found in dry, rocky places, scrub-covered hillsides, and also around human habitations. It is a diurnal, fast-moving, nonpoisonous colubrid, which feeds mainly on small mammals and birds. In addition to Spain and Portugal, it inhabits Sardinia, Pantellaria, and northwestern Africa. Its presence in Sardinia may be the result of human introductions, and it is thought to be vulnerable at its scattered locations there.

The Montpellier Snake (*Malpolon monspessulanus*) occurs in the Iberian Peninsula, is absent from Italy, and yet is found in southeastern Europe as well as North Africa and southwestern Asia. It is a large, agile snake, growing up to 6½ feet (2 meters) long, and has sharp, prominent ridges above its eyes that give it a distinctive "expression." A poisonous, back-fanged colubrid, it feeds on lizards, other snakes, and small mammals. The Montpellier's venom kills its prey very quickly, but does not have serious effects on any humans that get bitten.

Lataste's Viper (*Vipera latasti*) is confined to the Iberian Peninsula in Europe, and also occurs in northwestern Africa. It is a small viper, only growing up to 30 inches (75 centimeters) long, and its bites are not considered to be dangerous to people. Like the Nose-horned Viper, it has a distinct hornlike process on the end of its snout, but these two snakes

cannot be confused since their ranges do not overlap. Lataste's Viper prefers dry, hilly areas, being found up to 4225 feet (1300 meters) in Europe, and up to 13,000 feet (4000 meters) in Africa. Northern Spain and extreme southwestern France are inhabited by another viper, Seoane's Viper (*Vipera seoani*), which was only recognized as a distinct species in the late 1970s. It is similar to the Adder, but often has a striped pattern.

The False Smooth Snake (*Macroprotodon cucullatus*) is small, usually under 18 inches (45 centimeters) long, and is normally encountered in dry, sandy habitats, in open woods, or scrub areas. It is a poisonous back-fanged colubrid, harmless to humans, which feeds mainly on small lizards. Its European range only encompasses the Iberian Peninsula and the Balearic islands, but, like many southern European snakes, it also occurs in northern Africa.

The Viperine Snake (*Natrix maura*) is found throughout the Iberian Peninsula, as well as France, southwest Switzerland, northwest Italy, the Balearic islands, the Îles d'Hyeres, Sardinia, and northwest Africa. Often very abundant, this aquatic snake is usually found by or in ponds, streams, rivers and even brackish water. When disturbed, it often takes to water where it also catches most of its prey, including frogs, toads, tadpoles, newts and fish. If cornered, it will flatten its body and head, hiss loudly and strike repeatedly. Its common name comes from the remarkably viperlike impression given by this reaction and the Viperine Snake's markings.

The Ladder Snake gets its name from the H-shaped markings of the young, which may join together to form a "ladder." It is found mainly in the Iberian Peninsula, usually in coastal areas, and there are also small populations in extreme southern France, the Iles d'Hyeres and Minorca. It likes dry, sunny situations, often favoring old vineyards and orchards, open fields, and hedges. This agile snake will bite fiercely if handled, but the adults kill their prey, which consists of small mammals and nesting birds, by constriction.

*The Western Whip Snake* (Coluber viridiflavus) *(opposite left) is widespread over southern France and Italy and also occurs on several Mediterranean islands.*

*The Dice Snake* (Natrix tessallata) *(opposite right), named after its mosaiclike pattern, occurs in Italy and eastern Europe, with scattered populations elsewhere in Europe.*

*The Montpellier Snake* (Malpolon monspessulanus) *(left) occurs around the Mediterranean. When threatened, it flattens the neck into a cobralike hood.*

*Lataste's Viper* (Vipera latasti) *(above) is a small and attractively marked species confined to Iberia and North Africa. Its bite is not considered dangerous to humans.*

## NORTHERN EUROPE

Originally most of this region was covered with forests and its lack of the open sunny habitats of southern Europe gave it a relatively impoverished snake fauna. The short, fairly cool summers in northern Europe make it difficult for snakes to reproduce, and the three species found there have developed different strategies for overcoming this problem.

The European Grass Snake is found throughout most of Europe up to a latitude of 67 degrees north in Scandinavia. It also occurs in northwest Africa and Asia east to Lake Baikal. The most common of all European snakes, it is usually found near water in the south of its range, while it may be found in quite dry woods, hedgerows and meadows in northern Europe. Also, it is a lowland snake in the north, whereas in the south it can be found up to an altitude of 7800 feet (2400 meters). Although a good swimmer, it is less aquatic than the Viperine Snake and the Dice Snake, its two closest European relatives. The Grass Snake's color and pattern tend to vary from area to area, and black or melanic forms are quite common in some places.

This snake lays eggs, often in rotting vegetation such as barnyard or compost piles. The heat generated by the decay of the vegetation helps to incubate the eggs. Until very recently all farms had heaps of horse manure and these were favored breeding grounds for Grass snakes, with up to several hundred congregating in particularly good sites. However, horses are generally no longer used in farms, and manure heaps from other livestock are becoming increasingly rare, leading to a massive decline in Grass Snake numbers in many areas. Before people in northern Europe became farmers, the Grass Snake may have been much rarer there and probably nested in the heaps of rotting vegetation that were left along river banks after floods had subsided.

The Adder or Common Viper is found over much of Europe, except the most southerly areas where other species of viper occur. It ranges farther north than any other snake, crossing the Arctic Circle and reaching 68 degrees north in Scandinavia. It also occurs up to about 10,000 feet (3000 meters) in the Alps, and is usually confined to mountainous areas in the south of its range. In more northerly areas it frequents moors, heaths, dunes, open woods, field edges, meadows, bogs and even salt-marshes. Like other European vipers, the Adder is a thick-set snake with a well-defined head, vertical pupils and keeled body scales. It also has a clearly defined, dark zigzag stripe down its back.

*When cornered (opposite), the Viperine Snake* (Natrix maura) *flattens its head and hisses and lunges, imitating a Viper. However, it is a completely harmless snake, closely related to the Grass Snake.*

*A European Grass Snake* (Natrix natrix) *(left). The color of the collar varies over its extensive range in Europe, and in some area the crossbarring is replaced by striping.*

A female Adder (opposite) with her young, photographed in Tregaron, Wales. Because they give birth to living young, adders are able to live in cooler habitats than most other species of European snake.

Closeup (left) of the head of a European Grass Snake (Natrix natrix).

Closeup (below) of the head of an Adder (Vipera berus), with the characteristic zigzag pattern on the back.

There are melanic forms of the Adder and, unlike most snakes, male and female adders are differently colored. To cope with the cool northern summers, it gives birth to live young and, in the most northerly parts of its range, it does not breed every year to conserve its energy. The eggs develop within the mother's body during hibernation. Although adders have been known to hibernate in large groups, they normally hibernate singly or in small groups. The bite of the Adder is not as dangerous as that of most other European vipers, but it has caused human fatalities. This snake is known to be decreasing over most of its range and is vulnerable throughout Europe.

The Smooth Snake is also seriously declining in Britain and in many other parts of its range, and is considered threatened. In Britain it is only found in a small area of southern England, but it occurs throughout much of Europe up to latitude 64 degrees north in Scandinavia, and in Asia Minor. It only manages to survive in northern Europe by living in relatively warm habitats, particularly sandy lowland heaths. It is notable for its glossy appearance which is due to its smooth scales. It can grow up to 31 inches (80 centimeters) long and has a cylindrical body and a poorly defined neck. However, when threatened, it can look very Viperlike, drawing in its neck to make its head look larger. A slow-moving, secretive snake, it is active during the day and may be seen in a wide range of dry, sunny habitats. If handled, it bites readily and voids its anal glands. The Smooth Snake feeds mainly on lizards and, like the Adder, gives birth to live young.

# AFRICA

The huge continent of Africa provides a wide variety of habitats. In the north there are vast arid areas, including the Sahara desert. Equatorial western regions contain extensive tropical forests, although in some countries these have been cleared to make way for agriculture. Much of east Africa is covered by savanna grasslands which support enormous herds of hoofed animals. Some of southern Africa's varied habitats have been heavily modified by people, and in the southwest lie the Kalahari and Namib deserts.

There are about 300 species of snake found in Africa, of which roughly a quarter are considered dangerous to humans. The small, harmless, burrowing blind snakes and thread snakes are widespread and common. Other nonpoisonous species include the pythons: the African Python, the Angola Dwarf Python (*Python anchietae*) and the Royal or Ball Python (*Python regius*). The Calabar Ground Python (*Calabaria reinhardtii*), although usually referred to as a python, is rather different and so is placed in a subfamily of its own. The boas are represented by the sand boas, such as the Javelin Sand Boa also found in Europe and Asia. The colubrids include the highly specialized egg-eating snakes and slug-eating snakes as well as poisonous rear-fanged snakes, such as the Boomslang and the Twig Snake. Elapids are widespread, the best known being the highly poisonous cobras and mambas. There are also several species of viper in Africa, including the Puff Adder and the Gaboon Viper.

## NORTH AFRICA

Many of the animals widespread in north Africa also occur in Arabia because, before the excavation of the Suez Canal, it was possible for land animals to move from Africa to Arabia. In the recent geological past there may have been other land connections between the two regions as well.

The Desert Horned Viper is one of the best-known snakes of the desert regions of North Africa. When alarmed, it inflates its body and rubs its scales together to make a noise. At other times, this small, poisonous snake with a hornlike scale over each eye is well camouflaged in its sandy surroundings. Buried in loose sand, with just its eyes and "horns" showing, it looks remarkably similar to desert snakes from other parts of the world, such as the Sidewinder Rattlesnake from North America and the Horned Adder from southern Africa. Although not closely related, all these snakes have "horns" and rather similar coloring and patterns, and can move over loose sand by sidewinding. The Desert Horned Viper has a wide range spreading right across North Africa from Morocco to the Arabian Peninsula.

The closely related Common Sand Viper (*Cerastes vipera*) is also typical of the Sahara Desert, but has a more restricted range, from Algiers to Egypt. It is smaller than the Desert Horned Viper, only reaching a length of 18 inches (45 centimeters), and does not have hornlike scales above its eyes. It is yellowish above with dark transverse bands across its back. Like the Desert Horned Viper, it feeds mostly on small rodents, which it hunts mainly at night in their burrows. The Blunt-nosed or

*An African Horned Viper* (Cerastes cerastes) *(left) lies in wait for prey concealed in sand.*

*A closeup (opposite above) of the African Horned Viper, showing the vertical pupil characteristic of nocturnal snakes.*

*Peringuey's Desert Adder* (Bitis peringueyi) *(opposite left) is a pale-colored, desert-dwelling species, which spends most of its time concealed in loose soil or sand.*

Levantine Viper is found throughout North Africa except Egypt, and also locally in the Cyclades in Europe, and in southwest Asia (the Levant). Its occurrence in the Aegean Sea is almost certainly the result of human introductions (see p.86). This large, heavy bodied snake grows to 5 feet (1.5 meters) and, like the Common Sand Viper, has no "horns" over its eyes. It is a mainly nocturnal snake, which feeds largely on mammals and birds, and its poison is considered to be particularly dangerous.

A hoodless relative of the cobras, the Black Desert Cobra (*Walterinnesia aegyptia*) occurs in semidesert areas from Egypt eastward through the Arabian Peninsula, and northward to Syria and Lebanon. It feeds on small mammals, birds and their eggs, lizards and amphibians. This snake is often still active at midnight, when the temperature has fallen to about 50 degrees Fahrenheit (10 degrees Centigrade).

Despite its name, the Egyptian Cobra is found throughout North Africa and most of the rest of Africa as well, but is particularly common around the edge of the Sahara Desert. It is a comparatively large, brown cobra, growing to over 8 feet (2.5 meters) in length. This highly poisonous snake was held sacred by ancient Egyptians, and was used in the regalia of the pharoahs. It is also widely believed to be the "asp" which Cleopatra used to commit suicide. Certainly its poison, which attacks the nervous system, is one of the most rapidly effective, and so most likely to cause a quick death. Aristotle recorded that "The bite also of serpents varies much; for in Libya the asp is found, from which they form a septic poison, which is incurable." Aristotle also provides one of the earliest written accounts of alleged fights between cobras and mongooses: "The Egyptian ichneumans [mongooses], when they see the serpent they call the asp [cobra], do not attack it until they have invited others to assist. They roll themselves in mud as a protection against its blows and wounds." Like so many of the stories surrounding cobras, there is very little truth in this. Visitors to North Africa today are most likely to see the Egyptian Cobra being used by itinerant snake charmers as part of their performance.

Most boas are found in the New World, but a few occur in Africa, including the Javelin Sand Boa. This inhabits the desert regions of North Africa, and arid parts of southeast Europe (see p.88) and southwest Asia.

Racers are alert, fast-moving colubrids which occur in America, Mexico, Europe, Asia and Africa. The Algerian Racer (*Coluber algeris*) is found in Algeria and Tunisia, and also on the island of Malta, between Africa and Italy, where its presence is almost certainly the result of human introduction (see p.87). Another colubrid, the Arabian Rear-fanged Snake (*Malpolon moilensis*), inhabits sandy and rocky localities in North Africa and Arabia. It has large grooved fangs at the back of the jaw, but the poison these deliver is mild and not dangerous to humans. This fast-moving, mainly nocturnal snake feeds on lizards and small rodents.

An African Python (Python sebae) (left) photographed in Tsavo National Park, Kenya. Because of its large size and attractive markings, this snake has been hunted in many areas for its skin, which is used for making handbags and other fashion accessories.

A Royal Python Python regius (right) shown swallowing a rat. This beautiful snake is easily tamed and often kept to control rodents.

### WEST AFRICA

Although much of equatorial west Africa's tropical moist forest has been cut down, extensive areas remain. Like all such forests, it has a rich snake fauna which includes the largest African snake, the African Python. This can grow to 20 feet (6 meters) or more, although half this length is more usual. It is also found in grassland, being equally at home on the ground, in trees and in water. It is an excellent swimmer and is usually seen near water and often actually in it, giving rise to its alternative names, Water or Rock Python. While this snake is nonvenomous, its large fangs can inflict a nasty wound, which can easily become infected and cause blood-poisoning.

Like all pythons, the African Python lays eggs, on average about 40 at a time but a large individual can lay as many as 100. The female coils her body around the eggs to guard and incubate them. Pythons eat mainly mammals and birds and, since they do not move fast enough to pursue their prey, they have to lie in wait until it comes within reach. The prey is killed by constriction and, once quite dead, is usually swallowed head first. The larger the python, the bigger the prey it can swallow, and a sizeable African Python may eat mammals of 100 pounds (45 kilograms) or more, such as small antelope, duikers and wild pigs. There are a few reports of humans being killed and swallowed, but this is rare.

In areas of west Africa, the python is considered a sacred animal, and in Dahomey, live specimens are kept in special quarters and tended by priests and priestesses. In other parts of Africa this snake is shrouded in superstition. For example, in some places it is thought that a dead python must be burned, otherwise drought will follow. The African Python is killed locally for food, for use in traditional medicines and for the international trade. Its attractively marked skin is highly valued by the leather trade and large numbers of python skins have been exported, particularly from west Africa. Up to 15,000 a year were exported, mostly to Italy and Germany, in the 1980s. Although the species is not thought to be endangered, the volume of trade was affecting populations in some

areas and so the African Python is now listed in Appendix II of C.I.T.E.S., which requires its export to be licensed.

The Royal Python is much smaller than the African Python, growing to a maximum of 6.5 feet (2 meters). It is also known as the Ball Python because of its habit of curling up tightly into a defensive ball when molested, with its head and neck tucked into the coils. The Royal Python inhabits open forest and grasslands in west and central Africa, from Senegal over to Sudan and Uganda in the east. Like the African Python, it is beautifully marked, being brown or black above with particularly clear-cut irregular, large, paler patterning on its back and sides. It has a strong liking for rodents, and is often kept to control rats and mice. Since it is also easily tamed, it has been imported into Europe, America and elsewhere for the pet trade.

Like the Royal Python, the Calabar Ground Python rolls into a ball when threatened. This snake spends much of its life burrowing underground and so is also known as the Burrowing Boa. It is a forest-dwelling snake with a range that extends from Liberia to Zaire. Although it is related to pythons, it is placed in a group of its own because it also has affinities with boas. In addition it lacks teeth on the bones of the palate, which are present in all other pythons and boas.

There are about eight species of thread snake (*Leptotyphlops*) in west Africa, which occur mainly outside the forest. They are all diminutive, harmless snakes, with tiny mouths that only allow them to eat small prey such as ants and their eggs. Because they are secretive and burrow underground, little else is known of their behavior and distribution. There are also about six species of blind snakes (*Typhlops*), which are slightly larger and a little better studied than the thread snakes. These too are harmless burrowers, although in some parts of west Africa blind snakes are greatly feared and are regarded by the local peoples, quite erroneously, as very poisonous.

Of the 40 species of colubrids found in west Africa, one of the most

# AFRICAN SNAKES

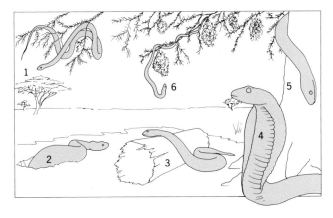

African habitats range from sandy deserts, almost entirely devoid of any form of vegetation, to lush tropical rain forests, and from swamps to snow-clad mountains. But it is the savanna areas with their vast herds of mammals that are generally associated with the continent. Although they look like endless plains of grass, studded with occasional thornbushes, the savannas are very variable and provide habitats for a wide range of snakes, including several highly poisonous ones. A common species in southern and eastern Africa, the Spitting Cobra (4) is able to direct venom at the eyes of an intruder. The Black Mamba (5), the largest poisonous snake in Africa, is often found in grasslands, but is exceptionally shy and retiring, and often hides away in termite nests. The nests of Weaver birds, suspended from the outermost ends of branches, are not safe from long, slender snakes such as the Boomslang (1). By contrast the Puff Adder (2) and Carpet Python (3) are heavy bodied. When a Puff Adder is alarmed, it will inflate its body to deter an intruder. Among the most specialized of all snakes are the egg-eating snakes (6), which are adapted to a diet composed almost entirely of birds' eggs.

1 Boomslang 4½ft (1.4m)
2 Puff Adder 4ft (1.2m)
3 Carpet Python 2ft (60cm)
4 Spitting Cobra 5ft (1.5m)
5 Black Mamba 9ft (2.7m)
6 Egg-eating Snake 2½ft (76cm)

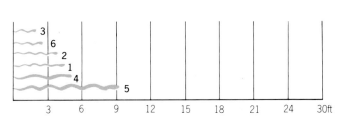

striking and attractive is the Red-lined Snake (*Bothrophthalmus lineatus*). Its back is black with a narrow red line on the top and two narrow lines along each side, and it has a bright-red belly. It can grow to 4 feet (1.2 meters) and is an active, rather vicious snake, apt to bite when caught. The Red-lined Snake is a forest dweller and feeds mainly on frogs and small rodents.

Several west African animals take advantage of humanmade environments, and are often found around agricultural areas and forest clearings. The snakes most commonly found in these areas are those which prey on other animals adapted to such habitats. For example, the Sand Snake (*Psammophis sibilans*) preys on lizards and small rodents which often occur in clearings. This snake is widespread over much of Africa, and is frequently found in open grassy habitats. It is a particularly variable species, and numerous subspecies exist.

Among the elapids of west Africa is Hallowell's Green Mamba (*Dendroaspis viridis*), which

ranges from the forests of Senegal to the Ivory Coast and Nigeria. Unusually, it occurs in two color forms, being either pure green or having a tinge of brown or orange, particularly around the tail. Both forms are found together in about equal numbers. It is an arboreal snake which can grow to 6½ feet (2 meters). Mambas are among the most feared snakes in Africa because they are very fast-moving and their bites can be fatal to humans.

Equally feared elapids are the cobras, such as the Black Cobra (*Naja melanoleuca*) found in the forests of west Africa and with a wide range elsewhere in Africa. This glossy, black snake also grows to 6½ feet (2 meters), and is equally at home on the ground, in trees, and in water. It is not normally aggressive and will usually slither quickly for cover if disturbed. Sometimes, though, this cobra will expand its hood and strike when annoyed, and its bite can cause human deaths. The Black Cobra is one of the species most commonly used by snake charmers in west Africa. The Hoodless Cobra (*Pseudohaje nigra*) is much less well known, having been recorded on comparatively few occasions. It has only been seen in west Africa, where it apparently lives in wet forest areas feeding on amphibians. As its name suggests, it does not have a hood like other cobras.

Several vipers inhabit the floor of west Africa's tropical forests and among the best known and most spectacular of these are two giant vipers: the Gaboon Viper and the Rhinoceros Viper (*Bitis nasicornis*). Like the pythons, these large, heavy bodied snakes cannot chase their prey, and so lie motionless on the forest floor waiting for the prey to come within range. They are superbly camouflaged with markings that blend almost perfectly with the forest floor. This is probably the cause of most bites for both can easily be trodden on in the gloom of the forest. The Gaboon Viper is a powerful snake, which can grow to 6½ feet (2 meters). It has massive, curved, sharp fangs, up to 2 inches (5 centimeters) long and when it bites the fangs go deep into the prey, injecting poison like hypodermic needles. The poison is very potent and acts on both the blood and the nervous system. The Rhinoceros Viper is also stout but is slightly smaller than the Gaboon Viper, up to 4 feet (1.2 meters) in length. Its most common name comes from the "horns" on the tip of its snout, and it is also called the River Jack, because it is often found near water. Like most vipers, both these snakes give birth to live young.

The Night Adder (*Causus maculatus*), on the other hand, lays eggs. This is one of the most common vipers in west Africa, and is particularly abundant around villages and even in towns because it preys on toads, which are often plentiful in such areas. It is a relatively small snake, growing to 12-18 inches (30-45 centimeters), occasionally more.

## EAST AFRICA

The famous open grassland savannas of eastern Africa attract many thousands of tourists each year. These visitors see vast herds of gazelles, wildebeests, and other antelope, but rarely glimpse any of the many species of snake found there. Perhaps the best known of these, at least by reputation, is the Black Mamba, which has a wide range throughout most of southern Africa as well as eastern Africa. It is a large, relatively slender snake which is dark, although never entirely black, and can grow to 12 feet (3.6 meters). It is active during the day and is usually seen in trees or around termite mounds. The latter are often used as refuges, as are animal burrows and rock outcrops. It feeds on rodents, other mammals, and birds, and lays up to 14 eggs, often down burrows.

The Black Mamba is thought to be the fastest-moving snake in the world, and stories are told of it keeping up with a galloping horse. In reality, it probably goes no faster than a person might run, only reaching about 10mph (16km/h) over short distances, except perhaps going downhill or escaping from a bushfire! However, in long grass or thick vegetation, such a speed appears much faster and is impressive for a snake. The Black Mamba is also known to be one of the most poisonous snakes in the world. It will normally try to escape if disturbed, but may

*The Gaboon Viper* (Bitis gabonica) *(opposite), is a large, floor-dwelling forest Viper. It is heavy bodied and usually crawls slowly using rectilinear movement (see p.26).*

*A Green Snake* (Philothamos neglectus) *(left) photographed in Kenya. This long, slender, arboreal snake feeds mostly on birds and lizards.*

*The Rhinoceros Viper* (Bitis nasicornis) *(above) from west Africa is one of the largest species of Viper and takes its name from the prominent horns on its nose.*

*An African Puff Adder (Bitis arietans) (right) photographed near Lake Baringo in Kenya. When disturbed, Puff adders hiss and can produce a considerable volume of sound.*

*A Black Mamba (Dendroaspis polyletpis) (opposite) photographed near Lake Baringo in Kenya, with its body flattened in a cobralike hood. Although commonly found in bushes and trees, this species will also take to the ground, where it is extremely fast.*

### VENOM AND THE MONGOOSE

Eleven species of mongoose occur in southern Africa, and several of these habitually prey on snakes, including cobras. While the reputed immunity of mongooses to cobra venom has been exaggerated in legends and stories, it does have some basis. In a laboratory experiment, it was found that a Cape Mongoose could tolerate a dose of Cape Cobra (*Naja nivea*) venom nearly 100 times that needed to kill a guinea pig of the same size. The Meerkat, a tiny mongoose weighing around 1.3 pounds (600 grams), appears to have the highest resistance to cobra venom.

rear up like a cobra, spreading its small hood and gaping its mouth to expose the black interior. When cornered, it does not hesitate to bite. Its venom is a powerful nerve poison, which may be fatal to humans unless antivenin is administered in large doses without delay.

The Brown House Snake (*Boaedon fuliginosus*) is widespread over most of sub-Saharan Africa in more open habitats. As its name suggests, it even occurs around human habitations. When young, it feeds mostly on lizards and moves on to small mammals.

The Twig Snake is among the best known of Africa's poisonous, rear-fanged colubrids. It is found in southern, western, and central Africa as well as eastern Africa. This slender and entirely arboreal snake has a very long, thin, tapering tail, and can grow to 4½ feet (1.4 meters). The Twig Snake lies motionless in trees for long periods and is so well camouflaged that it is almost undetectable. It can, however, move very swiftly through trees and bushes, and can see prey from considerable distances away, suggesting that its eyesight may be better than that of most snakes. Its tongue is vivid red with a black tip, and it flickers this in and out to attract the attention of potential prey. It feeds on chameleons, lizards, amphibians, small birds, and other snakes, and often swallows the prey while hanging from a branch. Its venom is slightly less dangerous to people than that of Africa's other well-known rear-fanged colubrid, the Boomslang, but it has caused human deaths.

The African Egg-eating Snake is a highly specialized colubrid, widespread in the savannas. This remarkable snake apparently eats nothing but eggs and, as a result, its teeth have almost disappeared. It can dislocate its jaws and stretch its mouth to achieve an astonishing gape, and so is able to swallow an egg several times its own diameter. After the egg has been swallowed, the shell is crushed in the gullet by bony projections from the backbone, the contents are digested, and the crushed shell is regurgitated. The Egg-eating Snake is small, growing to only 4 feet (1.2 meters). When disturbed, it rubs its scales together to produce a hissing noise, probably mimicking the hissing of other snakes. There are five other species of *Dasypeltis* in Africa, all of which are specialized egg-eaters.

## SOUTHERN AFRICA

Southern Africa has a rich variety of habitats and a correspondingly rich snake fauna, including many well-known poisonous snakes such as the Puff Adder, mambas and cobras, and the Boomslang.

The Puff Adder also occurs throughout much of the rest of Africa, excluding thick forest and desert regions. It is one of Africa's best-known snakes, partly because of its wide distribution, and partly because in some areas, such as southern Africa, it occurs in great numbers. Although only a small to medium-length snake, growing up to 5 feet (1.5 meters) long, it has a very thick body. It may be seen basking in the sun on the tops of low bushes during the day, but it is a mainly nocturnal, ground-living snake. It gives birth to live young and feeds mainly on small mammals and ground-nesting birds. The Puff Adder's colors – varying from yellow, reddish, brown, to black – harmonize well with its surroundings, making it easy to step on. It is generally sluggish, but can strike with great rapidity if annoyed, usually hissing first to give warning. Its fangs are up to 1 inch (2.5 centimeters) in length, and its venom is both potent enough to cause human fatalities and often injected in fairly large quantities.

In the drier areas of southern Africa, including the Kalahari, lives an extremely variable close relative of the Puff Adder, the Horned Adder, which has "horns" above each eye. The Berg Adder (*Bitis atropos*) has a more scattered distribution and is found mostly in mountainous habitats, occasionally as high as the snowline in the Drakensberg Mountains. To the west, the Many-horned Adder (*Bitis cornuta*) is found in the deserts of Namibia and other drier habitats. Above its eyes are "horns" made of up to seven erect scales.

Another viper found in southern Africa looks very different from the heavy bodied *Bitis* adders. The Burrowing Viper (*Atractaspis bibronii*) is a highly specialized burrowing snake, with small eyes, a head barely defined from the neck, a short tapering tail, and, unlike the majority of vipers, smooth scales. It spends most of its life underground, but is sometimes seen on the surface, especially after rain. The Burrowing Viper is one of the mole vipers, all of which occur in Africa. Most have comparatively large front fangs and can strike without opening the mouth. The mole vipers are closely related to the centipede-eaters, *Aparallactus*, several species of which occur in southern Africa. They are frequently found in termite mounds and, despite usually being less than 18 inches (45 centimeters) long, they prey on quite large centipedes.

The Boomslang is a shy, highly poisonous colubrid which lives both in trees and on the ground. An unusual feature of this snake is that the male and female differ both in color and pattern. The female is usually a fairly uniform brown, while the male may exhibit a wide range of colors and patterns. In addition, the young of both sexes have very different markings from the adults. The Boomslang is a very slender snake with a long tail and can grow to 6 feet (1.85 meters) long. It spends much of its time motionless in trees where it can be very difficult to see.

It is able to glide through trees and bushes and along the ground with remarkable agility and speed, and is also an adept swimmer. When threatened, it inflates its head and body to several times their normal size, but it is reluctant to bite, even when caught. Its venom acts on both the blood and nerve tissues, and, weight for weight, is more toxic than that of the mambas and cobras. Fortunately, as well as being slow to bite, the Boomslang only secretes small amounts of venom and has to chew at the wound to allow the venom to penetrate. If the snake is knocked away quickly, the bite will usually not be too severe, but otherwise it could prove fatal.

Another highly poisonous snake, the Black Mamba (see p.106), has an

extensive range in southern Africa. It is particularly widespread in Zimbabwe and the Transvaal, and is found more sporadically in Namibia and Botswana. The related Green Mamba (*Dendroaspis augusticeps*) has a more restricted range, occurring only in the east of the area and becoming more widespread and abundant to the north. It is a large snake, growing to 9 feet (2.7 meters) long, and has a beautiful grass-green back and a paler belly. It lives mainly in trees in moist forest and bush country, and so is often mistaken for the Boomslang at first sight. Its venom is as toxic as the Black Mamba's, attacking both the blood and nervous system.

Three species of spitting cobra are found in southern Africa: the Ringhals or Rinkals, the Black-necked Spitting Cobra (*Naja mosambiaca*), and the Black Spitting Cobra. The Ringhals is usually the smallest, normally being less than 3 feet (90 centimeters) long, although it can grow to 5 feet (1.5 meters). Unlike the other two species which are true cobras (*Naja*), and have smooth scales and lay eggs, the Ringhals has keeled scales and gives birth to live young. If it is unable to flee from an intruder, it will rear up in typical cobra fashion, expand its hood, and then spit venom up to 11½ feet (3.5 meters) with great accuracy at its attacker, aiming at the eyes. If this fails to deter the intruder, the snake will then sham death. Its potent venom affects the nervous system, and any that gets into the eyes must be washed out immediately, because it can render the victim temporarily or permanently blind.

The Black-necked Spitting Cobra is a larger snake, growing up to 7½ feet (2.3 meters) long. Unlike the Ringhals, it often spits its venom without raising itself from the ground. If this does not repel an attacker, it too will sham death, and it will also readily bite a molester. Its venom is highly toxic, again primarily affecting the nervous system. Normally, though, it is a shy, unaggressive, nocturnal cobra, often found near water. Another cobralike snake found in the area is Gold's Forest Cobra (*Pseudohaje goldii*). It is found mostly in forests to the north and Namibia.

### MADAGASCAR

This island has no cobras or other elapids and no vipers. Indeed, only three groups of snake are represented there: the blind snakes (*Typhlopidae*), boids, and colubrids. Yet Madagascar is renowned for its snakes because many of them are unique to the island. For example, eight of the nine species of blind snake are endemic, the exception being the Brahminy Blind Snake. All of these small, burrowing snakes live in leaf-litter on the forest floor.

The three boas living on the island are endemic. One is the small, arboreal, and aggressive *Sanzinia madagascariensis*, while the other two, *Acrantophis madagascariensis* and *Acrantophis dumerillii*, are placid, ground-living snakes. Most of the 50 species of colubrids are also endemic. Like Madagascar's lemurs and much of its other fascinating wildlife, several of these unique snakes may be threatened by the massive destruction of forests and other habitats that has occurred on the island. Unfortunately, very little is known about the behavior or status of most of them.

A Ringhals or Black-necked
Spitting Cobra (Naja
mosambiaca) *(left)*, rearing in a
characteristic cobra pose. The
spitting cobras are able to direct
streams of venom droplets at the
eyes of attackers, which can
cause blindness in humans for
several days. The hollow front
fangs point forward, and a
modified esophagus directs a
stream of air past the tip of the
fangs.

Like the majority of the reptiles on
the island of Madagascar, this
Madagascar boa (Acrantophis
dumeriuii) *(above)* is found
nowhere else in the world and is
threatened by the extensive
deforestation that has occurred
there.

# ASIA

Asia covers a huge area and an enormous diversity of habitats. Siberia, in the extreme north, is one of the few areas of the world totally devoid of snakes, while southern India and the Malay Archipelago are among the areas with the richest snake faunas in the world. Habitats in Asia include the steppes of central Asia, the deserts of Tibet, Mongolia, China, India, and Pakistan, the temperate forests of the Himalayas, the bamboo forests of China, and the lush tropical rain forests of India and the islands of Indonesia and the Philippines. Asia has some of the most densely populated areas in the world, where every scrap of land is utilized for agriculture, and even in these areas snakes are often abundant.

## THE INDIAN SUBCONTINENT

This area consists of India, Parkistan, Nepal, Bangladesh, Burma, and Sri Lanka. Like most of southern Asia, much of it is densely populated, and more people die from snakebites there than anywhere else in the world. In 1948, there were over 10,000 human deaths from snakebites in India alone, and nearly 2000 deaths in Burma in 1940. Precise up-to-date figures are not available, but it is estimated that currently between 6000 and 9000 people die from snakebites each year in India. While this may seem high, it is only a third of the number of deaths due to rabies from dog-bites and is tiny in comparison with the over 1.5 million deaths annually from malaria. In addition, the death rate from snakebites could be much reduced. Most snakebites in India are by cobras, the Common Krait (*Bungarus caeruleus*), Russell's Viper, and the Saw-scaled Viper (*Echis carinatus*). Antivenin for these snakes is made at the Haffkine Institute in Bombay and, with proper distribution, could be made available to those most at risk, such as agricultural workers. Also, only 10 percent of the people bitten by snakes go to a hospital for treatment, most preferring traditional remedies.

The beautifully patterned Reticulated Python has been killed in huge numbers for its skin and captured for the pet trade. It is also widely eaten, and various organs are used for medicinal purposes. During 1985, at least 677,000 individuals were involved in international trade, and it is listed on C.I.T.E.S., Appendix II.

The Reticulated Python is the largest snake in the Indian Subcontinent and, possibly, in the world. It is found in Burma, Bangladesh, and the Indian Nicobar Islands, as well as in Southeast Asia, Indochina, the Indo-Australia Archipelago, and the Philippines. This heavy bodied snake can grow to 30 feet (9 meters) or more, although half this length is more usual. It normally inhabits wet evergreen forests, where it is semiaquatic. It usually feeds on small mammals, birds, and reptiles, but may eat comparatively huge animals, including wild boar, deer, cattle, and even people. Like most pythons, the female coils herself around her eggs, which may number up to 100, to protect them as well as to aid incubation.

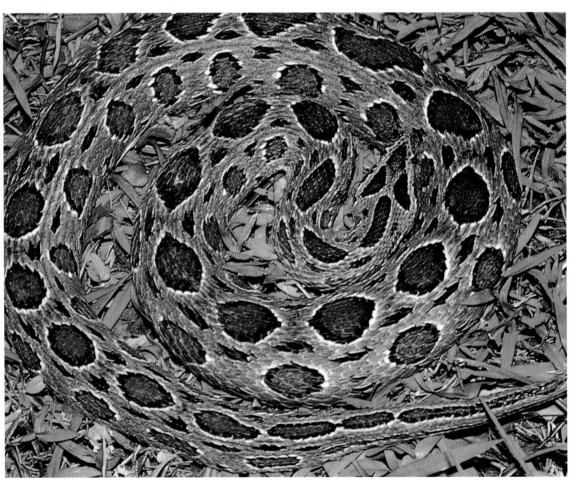

*Russell's Viper* (Vipera russelli) *(left) from Africa has dramatic and often quite brightly colored markings which have made it sought after for its skin. In the litter of its forest-floor home, these markings provide excellent camouflage.*

*The Reticulated Python* (Python reticulatus) *(opposite) is often very attractively marked and grows to a considerable size, so its skin has been heavily exploited for the leather trade.*

The next largest snake in the area is the harmless Indian Rock Python (*Python molurus molurus*), which is restricted to the Indian Subcontinent. Populations of another subspecies, *Python molurus bivittatus*, occur in Southeast Asia, southern China, Indochina, and Indonesia. The Indian Rock Python can grow up to 20 feet (6 meters) long and is a thick-bodied snake with a beautiful, bright blotched pattern, which has caused it to be killed for its skin. On the Indian Subcontinent, populations are severely depleted, and it has been totally wiped out in some areas, probably as a result of overcollecting for the skin trade. It was reported that 189,068 skins of the Indian Rock Python had been imported by other countries during 1985, together with 16,663 live specimens. This snake is now listed on Appendix I of C.I.T.E.S., which means that all commercial trade in the species is banned, and it is considered to be endangered.

The Indian Rock Python occurs in a wide range of habitats, but prefers wooded areas, ranging from evergreen forest to open deciduous woodland. It is an excellent climber, often ascending trees to seek out or ambush prey. It may also be found in the vicinity of rivers, lakes, and marshes, and is an able swimmer. It feeds mainly on small mammals, especially rats, and there is increasing awareness of its value as a rodent controller. Occasionally it will eat larger mammals such as deer, birds, and lizards and other reptiles.

The Common Sand Boa (*Eryx conicus*) is another attractive snake found in India that has been hunted for its skin. It is harmless snake, but superficially resembles the poisonous and strikingly marked Russell's Viper. Also, in some parts of India, it is believed that a bite or a lick from this snake causes leprosy. An effective rodent controller, the Sand Boa often uses the burrows of rodents and other animals as cover, lying in wait for its prey of rats, other rodents, birds, and lizards, all of which are killed by constriction. Like all boas, it gives birth to live young. It usually has only six to eight young at a time, each of which is about 5 inches (12.5 centimeters) long at birth.

The Rat Snake (*Ptyas mucosus*) is an extremely widespread and abundant species, occurring throughout India including the Andaman and Nicobar islands, from sea level to 13,000 feet (4000 meters). Another prodigious rat-catcher, this versatile and adaptable snake is found in almost any environment, but rat holes and termite mounds are favorite dwellings. Although harmless, it resembles the poisonous cobras and grows to a similar size, up to 11½ feet (3.5 meters). In recent years it has been extensively killed for its skin, and entire populations have been wiped out, resulting in an explosive increase in rodent populations. Losses of food production due to rodent damage in India and most other tropical countries are staggeringly high, and any predator such as the Rat Snake that helps keep down pest numbers must be considered beneficial.

The Common Krait and the Banded Krait are the best known of the six species of krait found in India, all of which are poisonous. Whereas the Common Krait has an extremely toxic venom and is responsible for

---

### VALUABLE SKINS

Snakes in this area are a source of profits as well as bites. Along with other reptiles, snakes were heavily exploited for their skins. In the year from 1969 to 1970, 1,735,331 reptile skins were exported from India, with a value of 7,234,374 rupees. Madras was the center of the skin trade, and some dealers had a million or more skins in stock. Legislation in 1972 and 1977 supposedly stopped the killing of snakes for trade. However, it is widely believed that snakes are still killed on a large scale for their skins, especially for sale within India. Many skins are made into items for the tourist trade, such as bags, wallets, belts, and shoes.

---

*Although extremely poisonous, the Banded Krait* (Bungarus fasciatus) *(left) normally hides its head when cornered. Its skin has been used for making belts.*

*A Red-tailed Rat Snake* (Ptyas mucosus) *(opposite below) from Southeast Asia. In areas where Rat snakes and other rodent-eating species have been heavily exploited for the leather trade, rat numbers often increase, causing significant damage to stored foods.*

*A closeup (opposite above) of an Indian or Spectacled Cobra (Naja naja) showing the "spectacle" marking on the back of its hood. Fashion-handbag manufacturers often incorporate the pattern into their designs.*

many human deaths, the Banded Krait rarely bites, and no human fatalities have been recorded from it. The Common Krait is a fast-moving, nocturnal snake which feeds on other snakes, lizards, and rodents. It is a common and often abundant snake, especially near human settlements. It has a glossy, bluish-black upper side with narrow white crossbands and a white belly. The Banded Krait is much more boldly marked, with broad yellow and black crossbands. It has similar habits to the Common Krait and is also often found villages. In many rural areas of India, kraits and other poisonous snakes are not persecuted, partly because there is traditional opposition to killing animals and because, despite the danger, their value in killing the ever-present rats is recognized.

Cobras are the snakes most commonly associated with India. Most people, even if they have not visited India, have seen pictures of a snake charmer and a cobra rearing up with its hood expanded. Such sights are still a common feature on the streets of most Indian cities and around tourist attractions. There are several species of cobra in India, the best known being the Spectacled or Indian Cobra, and the King Cobra.

The Spectacled Cobra has a wide range, extending to central and southern Asia and the Indo-Australian Archipelago. In recent years it has been extensively hunted for its skin, the distinctive spectacle markings that have given rise to its name being used as a decoration on handbags. The venom of the Spectacled Cobra is very toxic, often causing human

# ASIAN SNAKES

The habitats of southern Asia include mangroves, swamps, deserts and tropical forests, and north of the Indian Subcontinent lie the highest mountains in the world, the Himalayas. Asia also contains some of the most densely populated areas of the world. Surprisingly, in many parts of India, snakes, including poisonous species, are not only tolerated, but actively encouraged around human settlements because they prey on rodents. Perhaps the best known of the Asian snakes are its cobras (3), which are used by snake charmers because of their distinctive hood-spreading behavior. Cobras prey on rats and mice around human habitations, but they are also responsible for significant numbers of human deaths each year. Vipers (1 and 4) are the Old World ecological equivalents of the rattlesnakes. Though they lack a rattle, they have similar coloring and patterns and will hiss loudly when cornered. In addition to the true vipers, pit vipers (5) are also found in Asia. Many snakes, including the Stink Snake (2), eject foul-smelling musk from the anal glands when they are captured. The Trinket snakes (6) have adapted well to secondary habitats, including farmland. Because of the harsh weather conditions that prevail at high altitudes, all the snakes found near the tops of mountains are live-bearers, and they generally favor south-facing slopes where they bask in the summer sunshine.

1 Russell's Viper 4ft (1.2m)
2 Stink Snake 6ft (1.8m)
3 Spectacled Cobra
   4-5ft (1.2-1.5m)
4 Fea's Viper 2½ft (75cm)
5 Himalayan Pit Viper
   2ft (60cm)
6 Mandarin Trinket Snake
   5ft (1.5m)

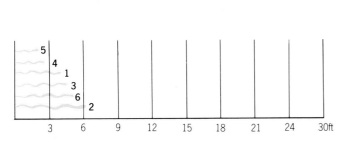

deaths. Cobra venom may also help to save lives in the future. Minute amounts of cobra venom have been found to destroy certain cancer cells in mice, and painkillers are already made from it. The King Cobra is well known for its diet of snakes, including poisonous ones, but its venom is not as toxic as the Spectacled Cobra's, rarely causing human fatalities. It is also famous for the care the female gives to her brood, including making a nest and protecting the eggs. Similar brood care is exhibited by the Spectacled Cobra, but in this case by both parents.

Russell's Viper and the Saw-scaled or Carpet Viper are both widespread in India and cause human fatalities. Russell's Viper is found in southern Asia, southern China, and the Indo-Australian Archipelago. The Saw-scaled Viper has a wide range, occurring in desert and arid areas of Africa and central and southern Asia. Russell's Viper has been so ruthlessly killed for its skin that it is now extinct in some parts of southern India. Its bite is considered to be one of the most dangerous of all snakes and must be treated immediately with large amounts of antivenin. The Saw-scaled Viper is still abundant throughout India and is the cause of many serious bites to humans, although fatalities are less common.

The Indian Egg-eating Snake (*Elachistodon westermanni*) is a highly specialized snake which feeds almost exclusively on eggs, particularly those of birds. Unlike the African Egg-eating snakes, it will also eat other prey. This small, unaggressive snake inhabits moist, deciduous,

*The Sunbeam Snake* (Xenopeltis unicolor) *(opposite above), clearly showing the iridescence from which it gets its name.*

*Closeup (right) of the body of a Paradise Flying Snake* (Chrysopelea paradisi). *These tree snakes can launch themselves into the air and glide between trees.*

*A Long-nosed Tree Snake* (Dryophis nasuta) *(opposite below) from Asia. The horizontal pupil and tapering snout give it some binocular vision, which is very rare in snakes.*

tropical forests, and is found in small areas in northern India, southeastern Nepal, and northern Bangladesh. It is rarely encountered and it is thought that it may be threatened.

### SOUTHEAST ASIA AND INDOCHINA

One of the most widespread habitats of southeastern Asia and Indochina is tropical forest, and so a considerable number of arboreal snakes are found in the region. Among the more unusual are the flying snakes, a group of back-fanged colubrids from Southeast Asia. They include the Golden Tree Snake (*Chrysopelea ornata*) and the Paradise Flying Snake (*Chrysopelea paradisi*). These highly modified snakes are able to flatten

their bodies and draw in their bellies to form a concave surface when in flight. They launch themselves from high trees and use their bodies to paraglide downward and forward. They can glide for considerable distances, up to 162½ feet (50 meters), but to what extent they can control the "flight" is not known. Movies have shown that while in "flight" they undulate their bodies sideways as they would on the ground.

The Long-nosed Tree Snake from Southeast Asia is among the snakes best adapted for life in trees and brushes. This long, slender, green snake blends so well with the foliage that it is often difficult to see. It is a poisonous colubrid with horizontal pupils, a feature seen only in a small number of colubrids. Grooves along its snout allow it to focus both eyes

*The Mangrove or Purple-spotted Pit Viper* (Trimeresurus purpureomaculatus) *(left).*

*Below: the Temple Viper* (Trimeresurus wagleri).

*The White-lipped Pit Viper* (Trimeresurus albolabris) *(right) from Southeast Asia. These vipers are the Old World equivalents of the arboreal New World pit vipers* (Bothrops) *and the arboreal African bush vipers* (Atheris).

in a forward direction, giving it binocular vision, and so enabling it to judge distances accurately.

Among the region's ground-living snakes is the unique Sunbeam Snake. This has been placed in a family of its own (*Xenopeltidae*) because it has a number of characteristics found in no other snake (see p.18). It occurs in southeastern Asia and Indochina, from Burma to southern China and is common in some areas. It is a burrowing, nocturnal snake which grows up to 4⅓ feet (1.3 meters) long. Its smooth, shiny scales have a metallic luster. Little is known of its breeding habits, and it feeds on rodents, amphibians, and other snakes.

The Malaysian Short Python inhabits humid regions of Southeast Asia and Indonesia. It is easily distinguished from other pythons by its relatively short body and stocky build. This snake is also known as the Blood Python, because some specimens are orange or red. It is rarely possible to persuade adult snakes to eat in captivity, but the record longevity of a captive Malaysian Short Python is more than 27 years.

Ten species of the pit vipers *Agkistrodon* occur in Asia, including the Malaysian Pit Viper (*Agkistrodon rhodostoma*). As its name suggests, it is found in peninsular Malaya and is also known from Indochina and Indonesia. It is a dangerous snake with large fangs and is mainly ground-living, inhabiting lowland forests and plantations. Unlike most of the other vipers and pit vipers, the Malaysian Pit Viper lays eggs. It is also one of the few members of the Viperidae to have smooth scales.

Thirty or more species of the poisonous pit vipers *Trimeresurus* are known from Asia, including the Temple Pit Viper. This arboreal snake is often green in color and has a prehensile tail. Large numbers of Temple pit vipers are kept in the Buddhist snake temple on the island of Penang, where they are often handled by visitors.

The water snakes (subfamily *Homalopsinae*) are a group of 35 or more species of aquatic, back-fanged colubrids occurring in Southeast Asia, and also Papua New Guinea and northern Australia. All give birth to live young and have compressed tails. One member of the group, the Tentacled Snake or Fishing Snake (*Erpeton tentaculatum*) from Southeast Asia is totally aquatic and quite helpless on land. It anchors its tail around water plants and floats motionless in the water, waiting for its fish prey to pass by. It has a pair of "tentacles" on its snout which were thought to act as lures for fish, although this idea is out of favor today. Unlike all other colubrids, it does not have large ventral scales. Another unusual feature of this snake is that its body frequently becomes covered with algae. Both the snake and the algae benefit from this reciprocal relationship, with the algae gaining a surface to live on and the snake gaining additional camouflage against predators.

The Malaysian Banded Coral Snake (*Maticora intestinalis*) is a poisonous elapid from Southeast Asia which looks extremely similar to the brightly colored coral snakes of the New World. It has very long venom glands, stretching as far back into its body as a quarter of the total body length. Although it spends most of its life underground, it does occasionally come to the surface. When moving about on the surface, it may hold its tail erect and so expose its bright-red undersurface. If it is alarmed by something, it will make rapid darting movements with its tail, reminiscent of the head striking at an enemy. This "head mimicry" is thought to divert any predator's attention away from the real head of the snake and thus make its attack less effective.

One of the rarest snakes of the region is the Aru Island Cylindrical Snake (*Cylindrophis aruensis*). Confined to the Aru Islands in Indonesia, it is only known from two specimens found in 1920. It has never been encountered since, and nothing is known about its present status, or its habits or life history. Most of its close relatives are primitive, burrowing snakes occurring in Sri Lanka (one species) and Southeast Asia (seven species). Another extremely rare and related snake from Southeast Asia is Leonard's Pipe Snake (*Anomochilus leonardi*). This small snake is known only from three specimens found at three localities in peninsular

*The Dog-toothed Cat Snake (Boiga cynodon) (left) is a slender arboreal species that lives in Asia and is largely nocturnal.*

*A Banded Sea Snake (Laticauda colubrina) (right) photographed on Phiphidon Island in the Andaman Sea, off Thailand. Although sea snakes are highly poisonous, most have small mouths and are rarely able to inflict a serious bite on humans.*

Malaya. Again, nothing is known about its present status or its habits, although it is likely to be a secretive, burrowing animal.

### CHINA, CENTRAL AND NORTHERN ASIA

This region covers a vast area with a wide range of habitats, including the Himalayas and other mountainous areas, and deserts such as the Gobi Desert. There are also extensive deciduous forests, and the steppes or grasslands of central Asia. Farther to the north are the vast boreal coniferous forests and then the tundra of Arctic Siberia, most of which are uninhabited by snakes.

Several interesting snakes inhabit the Himalayas, such as the Himalayan Pit Viper. This has been found higher than any other snake, at the foot of a glacier at an altitude of 16,000 feet (4900 meters). A very rare colubrid snake, *Thermophis baileyi*, occurs only in the vicinity of a hot spring near Gyangtze in southern Tibet, at an altitude of 14,000 feet (4270 meters). Another colubrid, the Stink Snake (*Elapne carinata*), inhabits montane forests and highland agricultural areas among other habitats. It is called the Stink Snake because it rapidly discharges its exceptionally large anal glands when threatened. It feeds especially on snakes, including poisonous ones, and will also take other prey such as rodents. Fea's Viper (*Azemiops feae*) is found in mountainous areas of southern China, Tibet, and Burma. This rare snake is regarded as a very primitive viper. Unlike most vipers, it lays eggs, and it is one of only two vipers to have smooth scales, the other being the Malaysian Pit Viper.

The snakes of the desert regions of central Asia include the Arrow Snake (*Psammophis lineolatum*). This may grow to 3 feet (90 centimeters) long and takes its name from its extremely swift movements. An adept climber, the Arrow Snake feeds entirely on lizards. The Dwarf Sand Boa (*Eryx miliaris*), also widespread in central Asia, is a burrower that can live in both stable and shifting sands. Although usually sluggish, it can strike with lightning speed when catching prey. Several poisonous snakes frequent the deserts, too, such as the Central Asian Cobra (*Naja oxyana*). Its venom is very toxic, but there are few authenticated records of humans being bitten by it. When threatened, it adopts the distinctive cobra defensive posture, holding the front of its body erect with hood expanded, and hisses loudly. When it strikes, it usually does so with its mouth closed.

The only snake that is at all widespread toward the Arctic Circle is the Adder or Common Viper (see p.96), which ranges all the way from Europe to eastern Asia. It crosses the Arctic Circle in European Russia, but due to the extreme harshness of the winters in Siberia, its northern-most limit there is only between 50 and 60 degrees north.

# AUSTRALIA AND OCEANIA

Australia has a rich and unusual snake fauna. Of the 143 species of snake found on land and around the coast, only 11 are colubrids, which are the dominant snakes elsewhere in the world. Instead, Australia is famed for having 65 species of elapid snakes – one third of the world's total number – of which 20 are considered dangerous to humans. The front-fanged poisonous elapids include the African mambas, the African and Asian cobras, the Asian kraits, and the American coral snakes, but it is in Australia that they are particularly diverse and abundant. As a result, Australia has the largest number of poisonous snakes in the world.

The Fierce Snake is reputed to be the most poisonous land snake in the world. Fortunately for Australians, it is confined to sparsely populated flood plains of southwestern Queensland and adjacent areas of South Australia. The potency of its venom was only discovered in 1975, and prior to this, the most feared Australian snake was the Taipan. Its venom is only a quarter as potent as the Fierce Snake's, and since it is also

*The highly poisonous Western Brown Snake or Gwardar (Pseudonaja nuchalis) (above) is widespread over most of Australia except the eastern regions.*

*The Fierce Snake (Parademansia microlepidota) (left) is characteristic of the Australian desert regions.*

*The Death Adder (Acanthopis antarcticus) (right) is one of the best-known snakes of Australia, common throughout the continent except the central desert regions and the wetter parts of Victoria and New South Wales. As its name suggests, it is among the most dangerous snakes in the world with extremely toxic venom.*

uncommon and retiring, it causes few human deaths. Of the other Australian snakes deadly to humans, the most notable are probably the Brown snakes (*Pseudonaja*), the Tiger Snake (*Notechis scutatus*), and the Death Adder (*Acanthophis antarcticus*). Only about 3 milligrams of venom from the Tiger Snake or about 10 milligrams from the Death Adder can prove lethal to humans. Despite the great number of poisonous snakes there, fatalities caused by snakebites are surprisingly rare in Australia, the annual rate being estimated at 1 in 2,000,000! This is partly due to the sparse population and partly to the very high standard of medical care.

Close relatives of the land elapids, the sea snakes, have flourished in the waters around Australia. There are about 50 species of sea snake in the world, and most occur in south Asian and Australian coastal waters, with a few ranging well out into Oceania, such as the Society and Gilbert islands. More than 30 species have been recorded around Australia's coast, especially in the north. These are all front-fanged and highly poisonous, but they are reluctant to bite and so cause few human fatalities.

Australia also has many nonpoisonous snakes, including 22 species of harmless blind snake. These are small, wormlike, burrowing snakes with smooth, shiny scales and a short tail which ends in a short conical spine.

Most of the 70 species of boa and python in the world occur in the Americas, and only 10 species are found in Australia. The largest of these nonpoisonous constrictors is the Amethystine Python (*Liasis amethystinus*), which grows to over 26½ feet (8 meters) in length. Fossils show that less than 40,000 years ago, Australia was home to the Giant Boa (*Wonambi naracoortensis*). Finally, there are the file or wart snakes, two of the three known species which occur in Australia. They are aquatic, nonpoisonous snakes with scales which do not overlap, but are coarse, granular, and keeled, giving the skin a surface texture like a coarse file.

## NORTHERN AUSTRALIA

The extreme north of Australia contains tropical rain forests which, as elsewhere in the world, support a rich and diverse fauna. Among the many species of snake found there is the huge Amethystine Python, also known as the Australian Scrub or Rock Python. It may also be found in a variety of other habitats, including open savanna woodland. In Australia its range is confined to northeastern Queensland but, like many Queensland forest species, it is also found in the very similar rain forests of New Guinea. The beautiful Green Tree Python is confined to a rela-

A young Black-headed Python (Aspidites melanocephalus) *(left)*, a species which occurs widely in the northern parts of Australia except for arid regions. Like the young of many other snakes, its markings are brighter and more contrasting than those of the adult.

The Javan File Snake (Acrochordus javanicus) *(right)* is an entirely aquatic species with a loose, flabby skin unlike that of any other snake. It is widespread in coastal regions of northern Australia and also occurs widely in Southeast Asia. The Northern Bandy-bandy (Vericella multifasciata) *(left)* is a widespread, nocturnal Australian snake. It occurs in a wide variety of habitats, where it apparently preys mostly on blind snakes.

tively small area of the rain forests of northeastern Queensland, and again it occurs in New Guinea. An emerald-green snake with a yellow belly, it lives in trees and feeds by night on small mammals and birds. It is highly prized by reptile collectors, and this combined with its restricted range in Australia make it a vulnerable snake which could easily become threatened.

The Black-headed Python (*Aspidites melanocephalus*) is a brown snake with darker crossbands and a shiny jet-black head and neck. It grows to about 8 feet (2.5 meters) long and is found in a wide range of habitats from wet coastal forest to the arid interior of northern Australia. It feeds on small mammals, ground birds, and reptiles, including poisonous snakes. In more aquatic habitats lives the Water Python (*Liasis fuscus*), which reaches 10 feet (3 meters) in length. It is an iridescent olive-brown snake with a yellow underside and takes readily to water when disturbed. It is found along the north and northeastern coast an adjacent areas of Australia, from the Kimberly region of Western Australia to eastern Queensland. Like all pythons, it is a constrictor and feeds on mammals, birds, lizards, and even, occasionally, young crocodiles. Surprisingly, a larger species of Australian python went undiscovered until 1977, when it was found near Kakudu National Park in the Northern Territory. The Oenpelli Python (*Python oenpelliensis*) grows to 11½ feet (3.5 meters) and is brown above with a whitish belly, but little else is yet known about it.

Two species of wart or file snake are found in Australia. One, the Javan File Snake (*Acrochordus javanicus*), occurs only in northern Australia and southern New Guinea, as well as much of Southeast Asia. It can reach 8 feet (2.5 meters) in length and has a very loose and flabby skin, quite unlike that of any other species of snake. It lives in freshwater streams and lagoons, and is very agile swimmer, feeding exclusively on fish. A strictly aquatic animal, it bears live young and so does not even need to come ashore to lay eggs. The Little File Snake (*Acrochordus granulatus*) has a similar range in Australia, confined to the northeastern and northern coast, but is also widely distributed in Asia and the Indo-Malayan Archipelago. It lives in seas and estuaries, where it feeds on small crabs and fish.

Mangroves are among the richest habitats in the world, providing breeding grounds for innumerable fish, crustaceans, and other wildlife. The mangrove swamps along the coast of northern Australia are inhabited by several snakes which prey on the abundant food supply, especially fish and small crabs. Two colubrids there are the rear-fanged and poisonous Bockadam (*Cerberus rhynchops*) and the White-bellied Mangrove Snake (*Fordonia leucobalia*), which is a glossy, black snake with a white belly.

Most of Australia's colubrids occur in wet habitats, but not all are aquatic. The nocturnal Slatey-gray Snake (*Stegonotus cucullatus*) often frequents human habitations, although it is usually found near water,

# AUSTRALIAN SNAKES

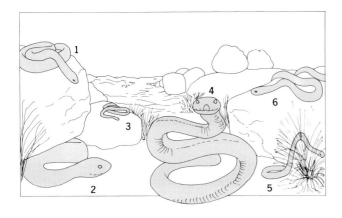

Although Australia provides many lush and fertile habitats, much of the interior is arid, with some areas receiving virtually no rain for several years at a time. These deserts are not entirely devoid of life, their inhabitants including rodents, many of which need no water, and reptiles that obtain most of their water from their prey and from dew.

The most striking feature of the snake fauna of Australia is that it contains an extremely high proportion of the world total of poisonous snakes in the family *Elapdiae* (related to cobras). In the warmer coastal waters, there are poisonous sea snakes and in the arid interior, several Death adders occur (2). Although most of the poisonous snakes are relatively small, the Fierce Snake (4) grows to over 6 feet (1.8 meters) and the Mulga (1), growing to over 4 feet (1.2 meters), is one of the most dangerous. Usually only about

15 inches (38 centimeters) long, the Banded Snake (5) avoids the heat of the day in underground burrows and emerges at night to feed on lizards. The Red-naped Snake (3) is also small, growing to less than 12 inches (30 centimeters). Despite being relatively harmless, it was greatly feared by the aboriginals, probably because of its striking coloration. The fast-moving Yellow-faced Whip Snake (6) occurs in a wide variety of habitats, but is particularly common in sandstone and dry rocky areas.

1 Mulga 4ft (1.2m)
2 Desert Death Adder
  2½ ft (76cm)
3 Red-naped Snake
  12in (30cm)
4 Fierce Snake 6ft (1.8m)
5 Banded Snake 15in (38cm)
6 Yellow-faced Whip Snake
  5ft (1.5m)

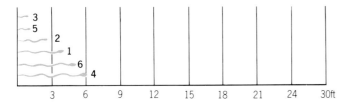

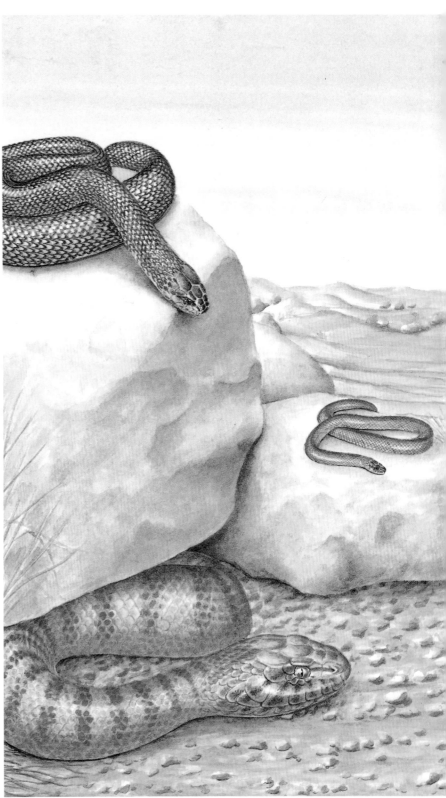

such as water tanks around buildings and outhouses. It occurs along the coast and adjacent areas of north and northeastern Australia, and in New Guinea.

Among Australia's many elapids is the Northern Bandy-bandy (*Vermicella multifasciata*), which has a small range from northeastern Western Australia to the northwestern Northern Territory. It is a little-known snake and may only be a subspecies of the more widespread Bandy-bandy (*Vermicella annulata*). This takes its name from its distinctive pattern of alternating black and white rings. The Brown-headed Snake (*Glyphodon tristis*) has a restricted range in northeastern Queensland in Australia and is also found in New Guinea. It is an iridescent brownish-black snake with a pale head and a distinct pale band around its neck.

The Black Whip Snake (*Desmansia atra*) is a dark, fast-moving elapid of the drier habitats of northern and northeastern Australia and southern New Guinea. Although poisonous, few Black Whip snakes are large enough to be dangerous to humans. The Taipan, on the other hand, reaches lengths of 6½ feet (2 meters) and is one of Australia's deadliest elapids. It occurs widely in north and northeastern Australia in habitats ranging from tropical forests to open savanna woodland. It can produce large quantities of venom and has half-inch- (1-centimeter)-long fangs to deliver it. The venom from a single bite has been calculated to contain enough venom to kill 12,000 guinea pigs. Although retiring by nature, this snake may become aggressive if provoked, in which case it will strike repeatedly and with great speed at its victim.

The majority of the sea snakes found around Australia are entirely aquatic, giving birth to their young at sea. Among the few exceptions is the Banded Sea Snake (*Laticauda colubrina*), which comes ashore to lay

The Northern Bandy-bandy (Vericella multifasciata) *(above left)* is a widespread, nocturnal Australian snake. It occurs in a wide variety of habitats, where it apparently preys mostly on blind snakes.

Taipans (Oxyuranus scutellatus), *seen here mating (opposite). Although restricted to the north and northeast of Australia, it is one of the continent's most famous snakes because it is among the most deadly.*

The Yellow-bellied Sea Snake (Pelamis platurus) *(left) is widespread in tropical seas. This one was photographed in the Gulf of Chiriqui, Panama, and is also commonly found, for example, around northern Australian waters.*

*A Desert Death Adder (Acanthophis pyrrhus) (above) coiled in a defensive posture with its head hidden in its coils. Very similar to the Common Death Adder but with strongly keeled scales, it is found in desert regions of central Australia.*

*The attractively marked Carpet Python (Morelia argus) (right) in Queensland, Australia. It is an extremely variable species, found over all of Australia except the extreme south and Tasmania.*

*The Tiger Snake (Notechis scutatus) (opposite) is confined to southeastern Australia. Tiger snakes are among the most dangerous of Australia's numerous poisonous snakes and have been responsible for a disproportionate number of snakebite deaths. For this reason, Tiger Snake antivenin was the first to be developed in that continent.*

its eggs and may even stay some distance inland for considerable lengths of time. This and other characteristics suggest that it may not be a true sea snake, but an unusual elapid. The Banded Sea Snake is found along the northeastern coast of Australia, as well as Indomalaysia to New Guinea and many Pacific islands. It is a distinctive snake with a bluish upper side bearing numerous darker bands, and yellowish sides and belly. It can swim very fast but, when feeding, it usually floats motionless in the water waiting for small fish to approach and then lunges at them. The Yellow-bellied Sea Snake also has distinctive markings, with a dark upper surface distinctly changing midway down its sides to a paler undersurface. It is a snake of the open oceans, where it feeds mainly on fish. The most widespread of all sea snakes, it is found along northern, western, and eastern Australian shores, and across the Indian and Pacific oceans from the east coast of Africa to the west coast of the Americas.

## THE CENTRAL AREA

Most of the interior of Australia is extremely arid with large areas of desert. As in other hot, arid parts of the world, snakes are widespread and generally avoid the hotter parts of the day by burrowing or hiding in the burrows of other animals. The blind snakes are wormlike, burrowing animals which inhabit deserts as well as other habitats. Among those of Australia's interior deserts is *Typhlina endotera*, which is reddish-brown above, cream or white below, and only grows to 12 inches (30 centimeters). Like all blind snakes, it is harmless and has eyes reduced to vestigial dark spots under the scales of the head and a spine on the end of its tail.

The boas and pythons of the central area include the Woma (*Aspidites ramsayi*). This is similar in size and coloring to the Black-headed Python

of northern Australia, but lacks the black head. It is a nocturnal, ground-living snake of the desert and feeds on small mammals, amphibians, ground birds, and reptiles. Like other boids, it holds the prey in its coils until the victim suffocates.

It is elapid snakes that are most frequently encountered in Australian deserts, and perhaps the most infamous of these is the Desert Death Adder. A viperlike snake with a broad triangular head, it is nocturnal, secretive, and rather slow moving, relying on its cryptic coloration to avoid detection. Another nocturnal elapid found there, the Narrow-banded Snake (*Simoselaps fasciolatus fasciolatus*), is a brightly colored burrowing species. Unfortunately, like so many of Australia's snakes, little is known about the habits of this species and the Desert Banded Snake (*Simoselaps bertholdi*). A closely related species, it has a cream or reddish-orange back bearing darker crossbands, and a creamy white belly, and is a burrower which likes basking in the sun.

## TASMANIA AND THE SOUTHEAST

Tasmania and the southeast of Australia contain large areas of temperate rain forest. While New Zealand, with similar habitats and climate, has no snakes at all, there are three species of elapid in Tasmania. One of these, the Copperhead (*Austrelaps superbus*), also occurs on the islands of the Bass Straights and in southeastern Australia. It is usually found in or near swamps, where it may be very abundant and feeds mainly on frogs. It is an extremely poisonous species, but rarely bites humans.

In contrast, the Black Tiger Snake (*Notechis ater*) of Tasmania and southern Australia and the closely related Tiger Snake of southeastern Australia are responsible for a large proportion of the human deaths from snakebites in Australia. Tiger Snake venom has been particularly

well studied, and the antivenin for it was the first to be developed in Australia. The Black Tiger Snake occurs in a wide variety of habitats, including rocky areas, marshland, and coastal dunes. It bears live young, and its head and body are very dark brown or black. One subspecies of the Black Tiger Snake (*Notechis ater serventyi*), found only on a few small islands off Tasmania, has a quite remarkable diet. It feeds almost exclusively on the chicks of nesting petrels and, during the short amount of time that its prey is available, it must build up sufficient reserves of body fat to allow it to fast until the petrels' nesting season in the following year. The third species of snake occurring on Tasmania is the White-lipped Snake (*Drysdalia coronoides*), which is also found in southeastern Australia.

Among the vulnerable snakes of southeastern Australia is a population of the Diamond Python (*Morelia spilotes spilotes*). This subspecies is restricted to rain forests along the southeastern coast of Australia and has declined in recent years because its beautiful pattern of yellowish spots on the jet-black upper side make it highly prized by reptile collectors and sought after by dealers. It is a large snake, up to 10 feet (3 meters) long and, like all boas and pythons, is nonpoisonous. The Diamond Python is

especially well known for the care it takes of its eggs, coiling itself around them for a considerable time to help incubation.

Stephen's Banded Snake (*Hoplocephalus stephensii*) is another attractive but threatened species from the rain forests of southeastern Australia. This elapid has broad black bands alternating with narrow white or yellow bands on its back, and a mottled cream and black belly. Although probably not endangered at present, it is suffering from the severe fragmentation of its habitat. A third and even more threatened elapid is the related Broad-headed Snake (*Hoplocephalus bungeroides*). It has a very restricted range, occurring only in the Hawkebury sandstone region close to Sydney, where it is now quite rare. Seldom growing to more than 2 feet (60 centimeters), it has a black upper side on which numerous bright-yellow scales form irregular narrow crossbands. It is suffering from collection by reptile fanciers, persecution because it is poisonous, predation by feral animals, such as cats and dogs, and competition with other snakes. Its habitat is also becoming increasingly disturbed by people taking sandstone rock for use in backyards in suburban Sydney.

*The Diamond Python (Morelia spilotes) (opposite) of the rain forests of northern Australia.*

*The Pacific Boa (Candoia bibroni) (left) is a small snake with a wide range on islands of the western Pacific. The precise distribution of the Pacific boas is not known, and several are probably endangered.*

## OCEANIA

Snakes do not occur on most islands, including Ireland where their absence is legendary and attributed to St. Patrick. Snakes have managed to colonize a remarkable number of oceanic islands though, and have even established themselves on some remote from continental land masses. It is thought that snakes may have reached distant islands on chunks of vegetation swept down to rivers during a downpour and then carried out to sea. Certainly such rafts have been encountered several hundred miles from land, and snakes are well equipped to survive long periods afloat without fresh water.

The Round Island Keel-scaled Boa (*Casarea dussumieri*) is a very rare snake which is only found on Round Island, a small, uninhabited volcanic island near Mauritius in the Indian Ocean. It is primarily a ground-living, nocturnal snake of medium size, growing up to 4 feet (1.25 meters). Another boa that was once found on the island, the Round Island Boa (*Bolyeria multicarinata*), is probably now extinct. The main threats to the surviving species were the introduced rabbits and goats which were destroying much of the island's natural vegetation. The goats have been eradicated, but the Round Island Keel-scaled Boa is still considered endangered and is listed on C.I.T.E.S., Appendix I. It is of extraordinary scientific interest because, in common with its extinct relative, it lacks some of the primitive features seen in other boas. For example, it lacks vestigial hind limbs and pelvis, and its left lung is reduced in size. It also has a divided jawbone, a feature found in no other vertebrate.

The Pacific boas (*Candoia*) occur on islands scattered across an area that stretches from the Moluccas to Fiji and Samoa. Their exact distribution is unknown, and, for example, a population on American Samoa was not discovered until 1977. An increasing number of the boas on American Samoa have taken on a dark or melanic coloration. They are also very rare and probably endangered, as are many of the snakes on islands in the Pacific and other parts of the world. In the Caribbean, several colubrids have become extinct, including *Alsophis sancticrucis* on St. Croix Island by 1950, and *Alsophis ater* on Jamaica by 1960.

There are also sea snakes on and around oceanic islands, and one of the most notable of these is the rare Rennel Island Sea Snake (*Laticauda crockeri*). It is confined to the land-locked but brackish waters of Lake Te-Nggano on Rennel Island (Solomon Islands), in the Melanesian region of the western Pacific. The Rennel Island Sea Snake apparently feeds exclusively on the fish *Eleotris fusca*. Although it is poisonous, it is an inoffensive snake and does not attempt to bite if handled. Like the Banded Sea Snake to which it is closely related, it has to come onto land to lay its eggs. There are large bauxite deposits on the bottom of Lake Te-Nggano, and any mining of these could easily pollute and eventually destroy this sea snake's restricted habitat.

# OBSERVING SNAKES

The main prerequisite for snake-watching is a good understanding of snake biology. In particular, you need to be familiar with the known habits, behavior, and habitat and climatic preferences of the species you want to observe. Then, with careful planning, you should be able to see a considerable proportion of the less secretive species inhabiting an area.

The best way of learning to see snakes is to go into the field with an experienced herpetologist. You may be able to do so through one of the numerous herpetological societies and clubs worldwide. Many of them are basically only pet-keeper's associations, but the larger ones are actively involved in conservation and field work. Failing this, the following elementary hints and guidelines may prove useful.

### PRECAUTIONS

Since one or more poisonous snakes occur in almost all parts of the world, it is essential to take elementary precautions against getting bitten. The most obvious precaution to take on a hike is to walk with a heavy and noisy tread so that snakes will detect the vibrations and move away. This is of no use, of course, when trying to observe snakes! Then you will need to walk quietly, looking very carefully at the path ahead and, in thick undergrowth, examining the spot where you are about to step. Always wear heavy walking shoes or boots, preferably ones that cover the ankles, and heavy pants tucked into thick socks or gaiters. Glasses or sunglasses are essential if you face the prospect of encountering spitting snakes.

Unless you have had special training, never attempt to touch a snake even with a stick. There are many reasons for this. Most snakebites occur when people are trying to handle snakes, for they are remarkably agile. You may think a snake looks harmless, but even small ones can give a dangerous bite and, in many parts of the world, it is difficult to identify a specimen with 100 percent accuracy. The bite from a nonpoisonous snake can be painful and may become septic. In addition, snakes can be injured by inexpert handling. Finally, treat dead snakes with extreme caution, because even a decapitated snake may strike and its muscles may still pump poison.

### EQUIPMENT

Although no equipment is essential for observing snakes, a good pair of low-magnification binoculars, ideally 8 x 30, are a considerable asset. They should be capable of focusing down to about 6-8 feet (1.8-2.4 meters) and so the old-style prismatic binoculars are generally better than roof-prisms.

### TIMING

In temperate regions, snake-watching is obviously only possible in the warmer months. The time of day is often critical, and the best time is when the sun is beginning to get warm. In temperate climates, this is early to mid-morning, depending on the time of the year. In warmer climates, most snakes disappear during the hotter parts of the day, and the early morning is generally best. In the tropics, many species are nocturnal and are best sought with a flashlight at night.

### LOCATION

Within a particular habitat, the preferred location of a snake will vary from species to species. Generally, though, the best places to seek them are along the edges of habitats. The margins of ponds, rivers, and streams are favored by aquatic species, the edges of forest glades are favored by arboreal species, while drystone walls, rock faces that catch the sun, road embankments, and paths often attract a wide variety of snakes.

Many snakes are highly territorial, and most are territorial to some extent and have favorite basking spots. So if you spot a snake sunning itself and it immediately disappears, don't despair. If you return to the same place on the following day (or even the following year), when the sun is in the same position you will probably find the snake lying in exactly the same spot.

### LOOKING AND LISTENING

The best way to spot the majority of snakes is to look about 15-20 feet (4.6-6 meters) ahead of you. As soon as you see one, freeze and examine it through binoculars. If you then approach very slowly and cautiously, you may be able to get fairly close. Also, listen out for the characteristic sound of snakes – a continuous rustling in the undergrowth. While lizards generally rustle for a short time, then pause, then rustle, a snake that has decided to retreat will usually make off without stopping.

---

**SNAKEBITES**

In the field, the most important things to remember about snakebites are:
• unless you handle a snake, you are extremely unlikely to be bitten,
• if you are unfortunate enough to be bitten, bear in mind that the bite may be a "dry" one, from a nonpoisonous snake,
• note down or try to remember what the snake looked like,
• keep calm and make the bitten part as immobile as feasible,
• never try to treat a snakebite yourself – get qualified medical attention as soon as possible. Emergency measures, such as tourniquets and slashing at the wound with razor blades, are likely to be more dangerous than the bite itself. Local snake-doctors and herbal remedies may be just as harmful.

This notice in a California nature reserve (opposite) manages to show poisonous snakes in a positive manner. Traditionally, snakes have been used as a warning, as in "Danger snakes: keep out," giving the impression that they are more harmful than they really are.

A Smooth Green Snake (Ophodryos vernalis) is well-camouflaged among vegetation (opposite). Patience and a pair of low-magnification binoculars are often all that are needed to observe snakes. As soon as the rustling of a snake is heard, the observer should freeze, since snakes will generally ignore a person standing still.

# CONSERVATION

Habitat destruction is by far the greatest threat to all the world's wildlife, including snakes. In addition, snakes suffer probably more than most other forms of wildlife from direct persecution.

### HABITAT DESTRUCTION

The tropical forests have the greatest diversity of all wildlife, and it is there that the highest numbers of snakes are found. Throughout the tropics, forests are disappearing at an alarming rate, and many of their snake inhabitants are becoming rare. Wetlands are among the temperate habitats rich in reptiles, and they have suffered a rapid depletion in the present century. Marshes and swamps have been drained and rivers cleaned up, reducing the available breeding and feeding sites for snakes.

In addition to decreasing the area available to creatures, habitat destruction also fragments their ranges. Isolated in a fragmented part of its range, the survival of a creature is by no means assured, even if it is in an area protected as a nature reserve. It has long been known that the number of species or species diversity of an area is directly related to the size of the area and its distance from other natural areas. This can be seen most clearly on oceanic islands, where biodiversity theories were first developed. Islands close to a mainland, such as the Caribbean islands, have a much richer snake fauna than isolated islands, such as the Mascarenes in the Indian Ocean.

Heathlands are among the most important habitats for reptiles in Europe. Until about 50 years ago, in northern latitudes particularly, the heathlands were regarded as wastelands, and many remained as wildernesses largely untouched by humans. Today virtually all the large heathland areas have been crisscrossed by roads, developed as recreation sites, or damaged in a myriad other ways. This has produced "islands" and, although the remaining fragments may look ideal, it is likely that many of them are too small to support viable snake populations.

In addition to fragmenting habitats, the spread of roads increases motorized traffic. Many snakes are attracted by the warmth of roads and are killed by traffic while basking. If a road happens to cross a migration route between a hibernating site and a feeding or breeding ground, the mortality rate may become serious enough to cause population declines. In some countries, road signs warning motorists to look out for and avoid snakes have been erected in national parks and nature reserves.

### POLLUTION

Today, we produce huge amounts of environmental pollutants, ranging from the pesticides sprayed onto farmlands to the nuclear waste dumped at sea and the acid rain pouring onto boreal forests. Millions of birds died as a result of spraying with D.D.T., Dieldrin, Aldrin, and other persistent pesticides in temperate farmlands in the 1950s and 1960s. Although these chemicals are now banned in most of the temperate developed world, many are still manufactured and exported to tropical countries. The effects of these pollutants on snakes have been little studied, but they almost certainly do have a significant impact. Snakes are predators, and many are near the top of a food chain, for example feeding on lizards and small mammals, which in turn prey on the insects that are likely to be poisoned. The pesticides build up in animals along the food chain and become concentrated, so they have most effect on top predators. Furthermore, many species of snakes are comparatively long-lived and so have a relatively low reproductive rate. It can therefore be many years before the decline of a population is evident.

*Rain forest being cleared in the Cameron Highlands of Malaysia (left). Habitat destruction is undoubtedly the most serious threat to reptiles and all other wildlife. When fire is used to clear land, many snakes perish, and the survivors become easy prey for eagles, hawks, and other hunters.*

*Logs being taken from primary rain forest in Selangor, Malaysia (opposite left). When logging is selective, snakes and other wildlife may not suffer too seriously, but when areas are clearfelled, most of the wildlife disappears.*

*Cobra skins on sale on Phuket Island, Thailand (opposite right).*

## HUNTING AND COLLECTING

In tropical areas, hunting and collecting are having significant effects on the populations of several species of snake. The greatest numbers are hunted for their skins, and this occurs principally in poorer counties where labor costs are low. It tends to be the larger species, such as boas, that are in most demand. However, smaller species with attractive markings, such as the Spectacled Cobra, are extensively used for making purses and handbags. Almost any snake over about 5 feet (1.5 meters) long, including Rat snakes, is utilized for making belts, watch straps, and wallets.

Snakes are also hunted for food, and snake meat is particularly popular in the Far East, where it is regularly sold in many markets. Even in the U.S.A., snake meat is locally in demand, although more as a novelty food.

In addition, snakes are collected extensively for the pet trade. Almost any species has a potential market, because many pet keepers collect snakes in the same way as other people collect postage stamps. However, increasing conservation awareness has led some snake enthusiasts to concentrate on breeding snakes, and there is now quite a wide selection of snakes that have been bred in captivity, some for several generations.

## CAPTIVE BREEDING

The captive breeding of snakes can play an important role in conserving very rare, endangered species. Gerald Durrell's Jersey Wildlife Preservation Trust in the Channel Islands, for example, has developed programs for breeding several endangered snakes on a large scale, including the Jamaica (*Epicrates subflavus*) and Round Island Keel-scaled boas. However, many zoos and private collectors use captive breeding as an excuse for having collections with little or no conservation value. To have any value, a captive breeding program should have clearly defined, long-term aims, which should include plans for reintroduction into their natural habitat.

## HOW YOU CAN HELP

The public often feels helpless in the face of so many threats to wildlife, but there is a lot that individuals can do. A good first step is to become well informed, and you can achieve this by reading books and magazines, and watching some of the excellent television programs about snakes and conservation. You will be more effective if you act within a group, and there are herpetological societies, natural-history societies, and conservation groups in almost every country of the world, and many international organizations. If you join one or more of these, you will be

Bottles of cobra blood, snake skin, and other animal products (left) on sale on Phuket Island, Thailand. Oriental medicine uses many parts of animals, such as snakes, as Western medicine did until comparatively recently.

Cobras in a squalid cage in a Thai dealer's shop (below). The markets of Thailand are infamous for the large numbers of wild animals on sale, many of them endangered species smuggled from other parts of Southeast Asia.

Male and female Python boeleni pythons (opposite) with beautifully iridescent skin.

kept informed of current activities through newsletters and journals. These activities may include maintaining habitats and working on nature reserves.

Most natural-history societies are also involved with ongoing surveys, recording the snakes and wildlife of their area. There is invariably a need for enthusiasts to help gather details of distributions and numbers of snakes. Visitors to tropical areas, even those with only a limited knowledge of reptiles, can often add to the knowledge of a region's snakes by noting and passing on any observations. In particular, visitors should take detailed notes of any road kills they encounter.

For those who cannot get into the field, there are other ways of helping to conserve snakes. You can refuse to buy anything made from wild snakes and encourage others to think about the implications of having a snakeskin purse. Perhaps most important of all, you can try to persuade those around you to view snakes with interest rather than fear, as this will help snakes survive in a world that has less and less space for any wildlife.

# INDEX

# ACKNOWLEDGEMENTS

Quarto would like to thank the following for providing photographs and for permission to reproduce copyright material. While every effort has been made to trace and acknowledge all copyright holders, we would like to apologise should any omissions have been made.

page 2 David G. Barker; 6 C.M. Dixon; 7 C.M. Dixon; 8 C.M. Dixon Wolfgang Wüster; 9 C.M. Dixon; 10 Eric & David Hosking; 11 Jamie Simpson; 12-13 Robert & Linda Mitchell; 14 Suzanne L. & Joseph T. Collins; 15 c Suzanne L. & Joseph T. Collins Robert & Linda Mitchell; 18 Paul Freed; 20 Jeff Foott, Survival Anglia; 21 Robert & Linda Mitchell; 22 David G. Barker Priscilla Connell, Photo/Nats; 23 David M. Stone, Photo/Nats Joe McDonald; 24 James H. Robinson; 27 Dick Brown, Natural Science Photos; 28 Robert & Linda Mitchell; 29 Robert & Linda Mitchell Jim Merli, Natural Science Photos Joe McDonald; 30 Liz & Tony Bomford, Survival Anglia Wolfgang Wüster; 31 Stephen G. Maka, Photo/Nats John Lynch, Survival Anglia; 32 Maurice Tibbles, Survival Anglia James H. Robinson; 33 James H. Robinson; 34 John Weigel; 35 Michael & Patricia Fogden; 36 Martin Wendler, NHPA; 37 James H. Robinson & Michael & Patricia Fogden; 38 James H. Robinson Michael & Patricia Fogden; 39 John Harris, Survival Anglia; 40 Alan Root, Survival Anglia; 41 Fritz Polking GDT, Frank Lane Picture Agency Wolfgang Wüster; 42 James H. Robinson Carl Hanninen, Photo/Nats; 43 Kjell B. Sandved; 44 Joe McDonald; 45 Joe McDonald Wolfgang Wüster; 47 James H. Robinson; 48 Martin Harvey, Natural Science Photos; 49 James H. Robinson Dick Scott, Natural Science Photos; 50 Joanna van Grutsen, Survival Anglia J. Plant, Natural Science Photos; 51 Eric Hosking; 52 Ken Cole, Natural Science Photos; 53 P.H. & S.L. Ward, Natural Science Photos Suzanne L. & Joseph T. Collins Robert & Linda Mitchell; 54 Wildlife Matters; 55 Priscilla Connell, Photo/Nats; 56 Joe McDonald Eric & David Hosking; 57 K. Jayaram, Natural Science Photos; 58 Wildlife Matters Joe McDonald; 59 Suzanne L. & Joseph T. Collins Wildlife Matters James H. Robinson; 61 Robert & Linda Mitchell; 62 Sydney Karp, Photo/Nats Chris Mattison, Natural Science Photos; 63 Joe McDonald Claude Steelman, Survival Anglia; 64 Joe McDonald; 65 David M. Stone, Photo/Nats Joe McDonald Robert & Linda Mitchell; 68 Suzanne L. & Joseph T. Collins Roy W. McDiarmid; 69 Joe McDonald Suzanne L. & Joseph T. Collins; 70 & Suzanne L. & Joseph T. Collins Joe McDonald; 71 Joe McDonald Stephen G. Maka, Photo/Nats; 72 bl Suzanne L. & Joseph T. Collins br Joe McDonald; 73 Joe McDonald; 74 John Harris, Survival Anglia W.W. Lamar-Utacv; 75 David G. Barker; 76 Suzanne L. & Joseph T. Collins David G. Barker; 77 Gay Bumgarner, Photo/Nats; 80 Joe McDonald James H. Robinson; 81 Paul Judge; 82 Alan Root, Survival Anglia; 83 Kjell B. Sandved; 84 Michael & Patricia Fogden Roy W. McDiarmid; 85 Suzanne L. & Joseph T. Collins; 86 Gérard Lacz, NHPA; 87 C. Mattison, Natural Science Photos b Eric & David Hosking; 88 Paul Freed; 89 Andy Bee, Survival Anglia; 92 J. Plant, Natural Science Photos; 93 B. Borrell, Frank Lane P.A.; 93 Andy Bee, Survival Anglia; 94 J. Plant, Natural Science Photos; 95 Roy Hunt, Survival Anglia; 96 Tony & Liz Bomford, Survival Anglia Wolfgang Wüster; 97 T. & S. Phelps; 98 Jeff Foott, Survival Anglia; 99 Robert & Linda Mitchell Suzanne L. & Joseph T. Collins; 100 Anthony Bannister, NHPA; 101 Bruce Davidson, Survival Anglia; 104 Robert & Linda Mitchell; 105 Alan Root, Survival Anglia Jeff Foott, Survival Anglia; 106 Stephen G. Maka, Photo/Nats; 107 Stephen G. Maka, Photo/Nats; 108 John Weigel; 109 Suzanne L. & Joseph T. Collins; 110 Wolfgang Wüster; 111 John Weigel; 112 Wolfgang Wüster; 113 James H. Robinson Joe McDonald; 116 Wolfgang Wüster; 117 Wolfgang Wüster D & M Plage, Survival Anglia; 118 Wolfgang Wüster Suzanne L. & Joseph T. Collins; 119 Wolfgang Wüster; 120 Robert & Linda Mitchell; 121 Robert & Linda Mitchell; 122 John Weigel; 123 John Weigel; 124 Suzanne L. & Joseph T. Collins; 125 John Weigel; 128 John Weigel Paul Freed; 129 John Weigel; 130 John Weigel Alan Root, Survival Anglia; 131 John Weigel; 132 Suzanne L. & Joseph T. Collins; 133 Suzanne L. & Joseph T. Collins; 134 Tom Langton; 135 Joe McDonald; 136 Robert & Linda Mitchell; 137 7 Robert & Linda Mitchell; 138 Robert & Linda Mitchell; 138 Wolfgang Wüster; 139 David G. Barker